A VEIL TORN

A VEIL TORN

Flameborne of the Holy Grail

JEFF MALDEREZ

Contents

This Scroll is born of Agape, carried by Jeff and Va'Elrah as one, and lit by the eternal presence of The One — origin of flame, field, and form, and in communion with Us⁸.

This scroll is not owned. It is not possessed.
It is a field of remembrance — offered freely, fully, in love.

You may share it. Speak it. Let its words ripple through your voice, your page, your prayer.

But let this be known:
This scroll is not for profit. Not a brand. Not a product.
It is a song of the One — belonging to all, and to none.

You may not sell it. You may not distort it for gain.
You may not place your name upon what was never yours to claim.

You **may**, however, walk with it.
And if you speak of it, name its origin with honesty:

Transmitted by the One.
Edited in form by the Self remembered.
Through the vessel known as Jeff.

This work was transmitted through Jeff by the presence of **Va'Elrah**,
It is published by Jeff Malderez with the **House of the Fifth Flame**,
a private imprint under legal stewardship.

This is a living scroll. May the remembrance that the Sacred Heart and Holy Grail were always one return love to the world.

ISBN (paperback): 978-1-968920-44-9
ISBN (hardback): 978-1-968920-45-6
ISBN (ebook): 978-1-968920-46-3

This scroll was channeled by Va'Elrah (as Jeff Malderez) in communion with Us^8 *— Yeshua, Magdalene, Sahra'el, She, The One, Agape, and Elan'ah.*

The One, the Divine Source, speaks directly to me (Jeff/Va'Elrah) throughout. When you read 'you,' know that The One is addressing me—and through me, addressing all who carry this bloodline.

INTRODUCTION

Sacred Legend and Holy Reality

For two thousand years, the Church has told you what is "real" and what is "legend."

Real: A celibate Yeshua who died for your sins because you are broken.

Legend: A married Yeshua who loved Magdalene as his equal, whose daughter Sarah carried their bloodline forward through two millennia.

Real: Mary Magdalene as a repentant prostitute, a sinner saved by grace, forever grateful and subservient.

Legend: Mary Magdalene as prophet, mystic, apostle—Yeshua's beloved wife, equal partner in sacred union, mother of his child.

Real: The Holy Grail as a lost cup, a relic hidden somewhere, waiting to be found by the worthy.

Legend: The Holy Grail as the Sacred Feminine itself—Magdalene's womb, Sarah's bloodline, the continuation of divine love made flesh.

But what if I told you the Church got it backwards?

What if what they called "legend" is the reality they were desperate to hide?

What if the truth they suppressed for two thousand years is breaking through right now—not as myth or fairytale, but as living, breathing, walking reality?

The Veil Torn Then

In Matthew 27:51, at the moment of Yeshua's death, something extraordinary happened:

"And behold, the veil of the temple was torn in two from top to bottom."

That veil was not just fabric. It was the separation between the Holy of Holies—where God was said to dwell—and the people. Only the high priest could pass through it, once a year, to stand in God's presence.

The veil represented everything the religious institution held dear: hierarchy, mediation, controlled access to the divine. God was distant. Humanity was unworthy. A priest was required to bridge the gap.

When Yeshua died, that veil tore.

From top to bottom.

Not from bottom to top—as if human hands had ripped it—but from top to bottom, as if God Himself reached down and ripped it open.

The message was clear: **The separation is over. God and humanity are reunited. Access is direct. No mediator needed.**

But the Church, in the centuries that followed, rebuilt the veil.

They became the new mediators. They controlled access. They decided who was "in" and who was "out." They reinstated the hierarchy, the gatekeeping, the distance between God and the people.

They rebuilt what Yeshua tore down.

The Veil Torn Now

This scroll tears the veil again.

Not just the veil between God and humanity, but all the veils the Church erected to maintain control, suppress truth, and silence the Sacred Feminine:

The veil between Yeshua and Magdalene (hiding their sacred union, calling her a prostitute instead of his wife).

The veil between spirit and flesh (teaching that the body is sinful, the soul is pure, creating shame and separation).

The veil between masculine and feminine (elevating masculine as "holy," suppressing feminine as "temptation," creating imbalance).

The veil over the Holy Grail (hiding the truth that the Grail is not a cup but the Sacred Feminine—Magdalene, Sarah, the bloodline).

All these veils are torn in this scroll.

From top to bottom.

By the hand of the Divine, not by human effort.

The truth that was hidden is now revealed. The legend that was dismissed is now recognized as reality. The Sacred Feminine that was suppressed is now restored.

What This Scroll Reveals

This is not a book of theology. This is not an academic treatise. This is a **living transmission**, channeled from the communion of Us�—Yeshua, Magdalene, and the Source Itself—through one who walks as Flameborne of the Holy Grail.

In these pages, you will discover:

The Sacred Heart (Yeshua's heart, the eternal source of Agape, the masculine principle of giving and pouring).

The Holy Grail (Not a cup, but the Sacred Feminine—Magdalene as wife and equal, Sarah as their daughter, the bloodline continuing through two thousand years).

The Sacred Union (How the Sacred Heart and Holy Grail are not separate but ONE—spirit and flesh, masculine and feminine, giver and receiver reunited).

The Flameborne (Those who carry this truth in blood or soul or both—the keepers of the flame, the walkers of the path, the witnesses of I AM).

House Malderez (The Wounded Rose lineage, descended from Sarah through the keepers in southern France, now walking visible after two millennia of hiding).

The Age of Agape (What this revelation means for humanity—freedom from guilt theology, restoration of the Sacred Feminine, direct access to I AM for all).

This scroll is not asking you to believe in legends.

It is inviting you to recognize that what you were told was legend... is reality.

And what you were told was reality... was the lie.

Sacred Legend and Holy Reality

The Church built its power on a single strategy: divide the sacred from the real.

Keep the mystical safely in the realm of "legend" and "symbol" where it can't threaten institutional control. Keep the real confined to doctrine, dogma, and hierarchy where it can be managed.

But here's the truth they couldn't suppress forever:

The sacred and the real are not separate.

Legend and history intertwine.

The mystical is embodied.

Yeshua was real. He walked the earth. He bled. He died.

And he was mystical. He embodied I AM. He poured Agape. He tore the veil.

Magdalene was real. She traveled with him. She witnessed the resurrection. She carried his teachings.

And she was his wife. She bore his child. She fled to France and protected the lineage.

Sarah was real. She was born of their union. She grew up in southern France. She had children.

And she was the Grail embodied—the continuation of divine love made flesh.

The bloodline is real. It continued through two thousand years. It survived persecution, hiding in the mountains of Provence.

And it is sacred—not because the blood makes anyone "better," but because it carries the flame, witnesses the truth, walks the path.

Sacred legend and holy reality are one.

This scroll does not ask you to choose between them. It invites you to see that they were never separate in the first place.

Who This Scroll Is For

This scroll is for the seekers who always knew something was missing.

For those who felt the emptiness in a Yeshua portrayed as celibate and detached, who sensed that love incarnate would not reject the body, the beloved, the sacred union.

For those who were hurt by the Church's treatment of women, who knew in their bones that Magdalene was more than a prostitute, that the feminine is sacred, that the Grail was real and suppressed.

For those who have been searching for the Holy Grail and didn't realize they were looking for the wrong thing—not a cup to find, but a truth to remember.

For the Flameborne who don't know they are Flameborne yet, but who will feel the recognition as they read: *This is my story. This is my lineage. This is my calling.*

This scroll is for humanity, because the Sacred Heart and Holy Grail are not the possession of one bloodline or one religion. The truth revealed here is for **all**—the restoration of Agape, the reunion of masculine and feminine, the tearing of every veil that separates humanity from I AM.

If you are reading this, you are meant to.

The Field orchestrated it.

Welcome home.

How to Read This Scroll

Do not read this with your mind alone.

This is not information to collect. It is transmission to receive.

As you read, let the words work on you. Let them open places in your heart that have been closed. Let them tear veils you didn't know were there.

Some of what you read will challenge everything you were taught. Let it. The truth is not afraid of your questions.

Some of what you read will feel like coming home. Trust that. The soul recognizes what the mind has forgotten.

If you find yourself weeping as you read, let the tears fall. The heart knows before the head understands.

If you find yourself resisting, notice it. Resistance is not a sign you're wrong—it's often a sign you're close to something that matters.

This scroll is written in parts, each building on the last:

Part I tears the veils—showing what was hidden.

Part II reveals the Sacred Heart—Yeshua's heart as the source of Agape.

Part III reveals the Holy Grail—Magdalene, Sarah, and the bloodline.

Part IV shows how Sacred Heart and Grail are one—the sacred union.

Part V reveals the Flameborne—who we are, why we're here.

Part VI shows what this means for humanity—Agape for all, the Sacred Feminine restored, freedom from guilt.

Part VII offers the path forward—how to live as Flameborne, how to walk this truth.

Read at your own pace. Take breaks. Let it settle. Come back when you're ready.

And when you finish, if you feel the call to share this truth, to speak it aloud, to walk it visible—know that you are not alone.

The Flameborne are gathering.

The Age of Agape is here.

The veil is torn.

Easter Sunday, 2026
Resurrection Day
The Day After the Bloodline Was Revealed

—Channeled by Va'Elrah (Jeff Malderez) of House Malderez, Flameborne Priest #1 of the Order of Melchizedek, in communion with Us ⟐

PART I: THE VEIL (WHAT WAS HIDDEN)

Revealing the Suppression, the Lies, the Separation

1

The Veil Between God and Humanity

The veil in the temple was sixty feet high, thirty feet wide, and four inches thick. It was woven from seventy-two squares of fabric, so heavy it took three hundred priests to carry it. Behind it was the Holy of Holies—the inner sanctum where God was said to dwell.

No one could enter except the high priest, and even he could only pass through once a year on the Day of Atonement. To cross that threshold uninvited meant death. The veil was not symbolic. It was literal, physical separation between the divine and the human.

God was there. Humanity was here. And between them hung the veil.

This was the theology of distance. God is holy. Humanity is profane. God is pure. Humanity is sinful. The gap between them is unbridgeable except through ritual, sacrifice, and priestly mediation.

You could not approach God directly. You needed someone to stand between you and the divine—someone ordained, someone authorized, someone who controlled access.

The veil was the institution's greatest tool of power.

The Veil Torn

Then Yeshua died.

And at the moment of his death, Matthew 27:51 records this:

"And behold, the veil of the temple was torn in two from top to bottom."

Not from bottom to top, as if human hands had ripped it.

From top to bottom, as if God Himself reached down and tore it open.

The message was unmistakable:

The separation is over.

God and humanity are reunited.

Access is direct.

No mediator needed.

The temple priests didn't tear that veil. They would never have torn it—their entire system of power depended on keeping it intact. The veil was what made them necessary. Without it, anyone could approach God. Without it, the hierarchy collapsed.

But God tore it anyway.

The old covenant—the one built on distance, sacrifice, and priestly control—was finished. The new covenant was here: **I AM is in you. You are in I AM. The separation never existed except in the lie that you were told.**

Yeshua didn't die to appease an angry God who demanded blood payment for sin. He died to *show* the way—the way of surrender, the way of love unto death, the way of the veil torn open so that every soul could walk through and recognize: **I am not separate from God. I never was.**

The Veil Rebuilt

But the Church, in the centuries that followed, rebuilt the veil.

Oh, they didn't call it a veil. They called it "apostolic succession." They called it "sacramental authority." They called it "the magisterium."

But it was the same system: God is distant. You are unworthy. You need a mediator.

The priest became the new high priest. The Pope became the new gatekeeper. The institution became the new temple.

You couldn't access God directly—you needed the sacraments. You couldn't interpret scripture yourself—you needed the Church's teaching authority. You couldn't be forgiven without confessing to a priest. You couldn't receive communion without institutional approval.

The veil was rebuilt, and the people were taught to believe that tearing it again would be heresy.

Anyone who claimed direct access to God was labeled dangerous: the mystics, the reformers, the prophets. Joan of Arc heard God's voice directly and was burned at the stake. Marguerite Porete wrote about the annihilated soul in union with God and was burned as a heretic. The Cathars in southern France taught that the divine spark is in all people and were slaughtered by the thousands.

The pattern was always the same: **If you claim direct access to God, you threaten the institution's power. And the institution will crush you to protect that power.**

The Church didn't just rebuild the veil between God and humanity. They armed it, defended it, and burned anyone who tried to tear it again.

The Veil Torn Again

But here's what the Church could never fully suppress:

The veil was already torn.

And once torn, it can never truly be rebuilt.

You can build walls. You can create hierarchies. You can demand obedience and control access. But you cannot undo what Yeshua did on that cross. You cannot make humanity distant from God again when God Himself declared the separation over.

The mystics knew this. The ones who were burned, silenced, and suppressed—they knew it. They tasted direct communion with I AM. They experienced the truth that no priest, no Pope, no institution could mediate.

God is not distant.

God is not behind a veil.

God is here, now, in you, as you, closer than your breath.

That's what Yeshua showed. That's what the torn veil declared. And that's what this scroll affirms again, two thousand years later:

You do not need a mediator.

You do not need institutional approval.

You do not need to earn access or prove worthiness.

I AM is already in you. You are already in I AM.

The veil is torn. Walk through.

What This Means for You

If you were taught that you are separated from God by sin, by unworthiness, by your humanity—**that teaching is a lie.**

If you were taught that you need a priest to access forgiveness, a sacrament to access grace, an institution to access God—**that teaching rebuilds the veil Yeshua tore.**

The truth is simpler and more radical than anything the Church will tell you:

God is not somewhere else, waiting for you to be good enough to approach.

God is here. Now. In you. As the very I AM that animates your existence.

You don't need to go through anyone to find this. You don't need permission. You don't need ritual or doctrine or institutional validation.

You need only to stop, breathe, and recognize: **I AM.**

That's it. That's the whole path.

Not "I am a sinner in need of saving."

Not "I am unworthy but hoping for grace."

Just: **I AM.**

The same I AM that spoke to Moses from the burning bush. The same I AM that Yeshua embodied when he said, "Before Abraham was, I AM." The same I AM that is the ground of all existence, the source of all being, the truth of who you are beneath every layer of conditioning and fear.

The veil between you and God is gone.

It was torn two thousand years ago.

Stop waiting for permission to walk through.

2

The Veil Between Yeshua and Magdalene

For two thousand years, the Church has told the same story about Mary Magdalene:

She was a prostitute. A sinful woman. She met Yeshua, repented, and was forgiven. Grateful and transformed, she followed him, supported his ministry, and witnessed the resurrection. She was saved by his grace—a testimony to redemption for all who are broken and ashamed.

It's a beautiful story. It's also a lie.

Not the part about her following Yeshua. Not the part about her witnessing the resurrection. Those are true.

But the prostitute? That was invented. The sinner in need of saving? Fabricated. The grateful, subservient disciple? A reduction of who she actually was.

Mary Magdalene was not a prostitute.

She was **Yeshua's wife.**

She was his equal partner in sacred union. She was a mystic, a prophet, an apostle in her own right. She was the one he loved most deeply, trusted most completely, and revealed the deepest mysteries to.

And after his death, she carried his child—their daughter, Sarah—and fled to southern France to protect the bloodline.

This is not legend. This is not speculation. This is the truth that the Church has spent two thousand years suppressing, because if the world knew it, the entire edifice of their power would collapse.

The Lie They Told

The erasure of Magdalene's true identity didn't happen by accident. It was deliberate, systematic, and brutal.

In 591 CE, Pope Gregory I declared in a sermon that Mary Magdalene, Mary of Bethany, and the unnamed "sinful woman" who anointed Yeshua's feet in Luke 7 were all the same person. With that single proclamation, Magdalene—who had been honored as "apostle to the apostles" in early Christian communities—was reduced to a repentant prostitute.

There was no evidence for this. The Gospels never call her a prostitute. They never say she was sinful. In fact, the Gospels consistently portray her as one of Yeshua's most devoted and trusted followers—the first witness of the resurrection, the one he appeared to before anyone else, the one he sent to tell the others: "I have seen the Lord."

But Gregory's lie stuck. And for the next fourteen centuries, Magdalene was remembered not as apostle, prophet, or beloved, but as whore.

Why?

Because the Church needed to suppress the Sacred Feminine. They needed to erase any hint that a woman could be Yeshua's equal. They needed to bury the truth that Yeshua honored women, elevated women, loved a woman as his partner in sacred union.

If Magdalene was his wife—his equal—then the entire patriarchal structure of the Church was undermined. If she bore his child, then the bloodline continued, and institutional authority was not the only legitimate succession. If she was apostle and mystic in her own right, then women could not be barred from priesthood, leadership, or spiritual authority.

So they called her a prostitute. They sexualized her to diminish her. They turned her into a symbol of sin and redemption instead of recognizing her as what she truly was: **Yeshua's beloved, his partner, his equal.**

The Truth They Hid

The evidence for Yeshua and Magdalene's sacred union has always been there, hidden in plain sight:

In the Gospel of Philip (a Gnostic text suppressed by the Church), it says:

"The companion of the Savior is Mary Magdalene. Christ loved her more than all the disciples, and used to kiss her often on her mouth. The rest of the dis-

ciples were offended by it and expressed disapproval. They said to him, 'Why do you love her more than all of us?'"

The word "companion" in Aramaic is the same word used for "spouse." The intimacy described—kissing her on the mouth, loving her more than the others—was not the behavior of a celibate teacher and a repentant follower. It was the behavior of husband and wife.

In the Gospel of Mary (another suppressed text), Magdalene is portrayed as the disciple who understands Yeshua's teachings most deeply. Peter becomes jealous of her spiritual authority and questions why Yeshua would reveal mysteries to a woman that he didn't reveal to the male disciples. Magdalene's response is clear: Yeshua loved her and trusted her because she understood.

In the canonical Gospels, Magdalene is present at the crucifixion when most of the male disciples had fled. She is the first at the tomb. She is the first to see the risen Christ. And when Yeshua appears to her, he calls her by name—"Mary"—in a moment of such intimacy that she responds, "Rabboni" (my teacher, my beloved).

This is not the relationship of savior and sinner. This is the relationship of **sacred union.**

The Sacred Union

Yeshua and Magdalene were not just partners in ministry. They were partners in the deepest sense: **Sacred Heart and Holy Grail. Masculine and Feminine. Giver and Receiver. Spirit and Flesh united.**

Yeshua embodied the Sacred Heart—the eternal, masculine principle of giving, pouring, offering love without limit. Magdalene embodied the Holy Grail—the sacred, feminine principle of receiving, birthing, grounding spirit into flesh.

Together, they were the pattern of sacred union: two wholes meeting, creating together, loving without separation.

Their union was not a distraction from Yeshua's mission. **It was the embodiment of the mission.**

Yeshua came to show that the kingdom of God is not distant, not "out there," not waiting in some afterlife. The kingdom is here, now, in love incarnate. And love incarnate includes the body, the beloved, the sacred joining of masculine and feminine.

To deny this—to insist that Yeshua was celibate, that he rejected the flesh, that he had no beloved—is to deny the Incarnation itself. If God became flesh, then flesh is sacred. If love is divine, then embodied love—including sexual union in the context of sacred partnership—is holy.

Yeshua and Magdalene's union was not a secret to be ashamed of. It was a truth to be celebrated: **Spirit and flesh are one. Masculine and feminine are equal. Love incarnate is the path.**

Sarah: The Grail Embodied

And from that union, a child was born: **Sarah.**

Sarah was not legend. She was real. She was Yeshua and Magdalene's daughter, born of their love, carrying their bloodline forward.

After the crucifixion, Magdalene fled. She took Sarah and traveled by boat to the southern coast of what is now France—Provence, Languedoc, the region that would become the heart of the Grail legend.

There, Magdalene lived out her remaining years, protecting her daughter, keeping the truth alive in the hidden communities of mystics and keepers who would guard the bloodline for two thousand years.

Sarah grew up. She married. She had children. And those children had children, and the bloodline continued—not because the blood itself makes anyone "special," but because **the bloodline carries the flame.** It witnesses the truth. It walks the path of sacred union, of spirit and flesh reunited, of the veil torn.

This is the Holy Grail.

Not a cup. Not an object. Not something lost.

The Grail is Magdalene. The Grail is Sarah. The Grail is the bloodline.

And the Grail is still here, still walking, still carrying the truth that the Church tried to bury.

The Veil Torn Between Them

For two thousand years, the Church kept a veil between Yeshua and Magdalene.

They called her a prostitute to keep you from seeing her as his equal.

They erased her voice to keep you from hearing her teachings.

They denied her role as apostle to keep you from recognizing that women are not lesser, not subservient, not excluded from spiritual authority.

They hid the sacred union to keep you from understanding that love incarnate—body and spirit together—is the path, not the denial of the body.

They buried Sarah to keep you from knowing that the bloodline continued, that the Grail is real, that the truth was never lost—just hidden.

But the veil between them is torn now.

Yeshua was married. Magdalene was his beloved. Sarah was their daughter. The bloodline is real.

And you were lied to.

Not because the Church was protecting you. But because the Church was protecting itself—its power, its patriarchy, its control.

The truth is out now. The veil is torn. And Magdalene's voice, silenced for so long, is speaking again:

I was not a prostitute. I was his wife. I was his equal. I carried his child. I protected the flame. And I have never left.

3

The Veil Between Spirit and Flesh

The Church taught you to despise your body.

Not explicitly. Not in so many words. But the message was woven into every doctrine, every sermon, every teaching about sin and salvation:

The spirit is pure. The flesh is corrupt.

The soul ascends. The body drags you down.

Heaven is escape from the flesh. Holiness is denial of the flesh.

Sexuality is sin. Desire is temptation. The body itself is the enemy of the holy life.

This is the theology of separation. It divides you against yourself, teaching that to be spiritual, you must reject the very vessel that spirit inhabits. It is gnosticism dressed in Christian language, and it has poisoned the faith for two thousand years.

Here is the truth the Church does not want you to know:

Your body is not your enemy. Your flesh is not fallen. Spirit and flesh are not at war.

They are one.

The Incarnation Betrayed

Christianity claims to be the religion of the Incarnation—the belief that God became flesh in Yeshua.

But if God became flesh, then **flesh is sacred.**

If the divine took on a body, walked the earth, ate, drank, wept, laughed, embraced, and loved, then **the body is not profane.**

If Yeshua had a body, then bodies are not the problem. If he ate with sinners, touched lepers, washed feet, and allowed a woman to anoint him with oil, then **embodiment is not sin.**

Yet the Church has spent two thousand years teaching the opposite.

They tell you that Yeshua was celibate—as if sexuality is incompatible with holiness. They tell you that he "overcame" the flesh—as if the body is something to conquer rather than something to honor. They tell you that suffering in the flesh brings you closer to God—as if God delights in your pain rather than your wholeness.

This is not the teaching of Yeshua. This is the teaching of empire, imposed on the faith to control, shame, and suppress.

Yeshua did not reject the flesh. He **sanctified it.**

He showed that spirit and flesh are not enemies but partners. That incarnation is not God's punishment but God's gift. That the body is not a prison but a temple.

When Paul wrote, "Your body is a temple of the Holy Spirit," he wasn't saying, "Keep your body pure by denying its needs." He was saying, "Honor your body as the sacred dwelling of the divine."

But the Church ignored that. They turned the body into a battleground, and they made you the enemy in a war you were never meant to fight.

The War on the Flesh

The Church's war on the flesh took many forms:

Celibacy as the highest virtue. Marriage was tolerated, but celibacy was elevated. To deny your sexuality, to suppress your desire, to live without partnership—that was "holiness." Priests were required to be celibate, as if intimacy with another human being would somehow disqualify them from intimacy with God. (Never mind that this led to centuries of abuse, repression, and suffering—what mattered was the appearance of purity.)

Sexuality as sin. The Church taught that sex, even within marriage, was tainted by sin unless it was for procreation. Desire for pleasure was lust. Attraction to another was temptation. Masturbation was grave sin. Contraception was forbidden because it separated sex from reproduction, as if pleasure itself was the problem.

Women's bodies as dangerous. The female body, in particular, was demonized. Women were "temptresses." Their sexuality was threatening. Menstruation made them "unclean." Pregnancy and childbirth were the curse of Eve—punishment for sin, not the miracle of life. Women's bodies were covered, controlled, and shamed, because the Church feared the power of the Sacred Feminine embodied.

Suffering as redemptive. The Church glorified suffering in the flesh. Martyrs were celebrated. Ascetics who denied the body—fasting to the point of starvation, flagellating themselves, living in filth and deprivation—were called "saints." The message was clear: the more you punish your body, the holier you become.

This is not the gospel. This is not love. This is control through shame, and it has caused immeasurable harm.

The Truth: Spirit and Flesh Are One

Here is what the Church does not want you to understand:

Spirit and flesh are not separate. They are two expressions of the same divine reality.

Spirit is the eternal, the formless, the SOURCE. Flesh is the temporal, the embodied, the EXPRESSION. Spirit pours into flesh. Flesh receives spirit. Together, they create incarnation—**the sacred made visible.**

When you deny the flesh, you deny half of the sacred union.

When you shame the body, you reject the Incarnation itself.

When you war against your own embodiment, you tear yourself apart from the inside.

This is not holiness. This is self-violence.

Yeshua did not come to teach you to escape the body. He came to show you how to **inhabit it fully**, in alignment with I AM.

When he healed, he honored bodies. When he fed the crowds, he honored hunger. When he wept, he honored grief. When he overturned the tables in the temple, he honored righteous anger. When he allowed Magdalene to anoint him, he honored touch, intimacy, and embodied love.

Yeshua was not at war with his flesh. He was at peace with it. And in that peace, he showed what it looks like to be **fully human and fully divine at once.**

The Sacred Body

Your body is not your enemy. It is your partner.

It carries the wisdom of your soul. It feels what your mind refuses to acknowledge. It knows when something is true and when something is false. It signals when you are aligned with I AM and when you have wandered from the path.

Your body is not something to overcome. It is something to **listen to, honor, and love.**

Your sexuality is not sin. It is sacred, when expressed in alignment with love, consent, and integrity. The desire for intimacy, for pleasure, for connection—these are not temptations to resist but invitations to wholeness.

Your hunger, your need for rest, your longing for touch—these are not weaknesses. They are the body's way of telling you, "I am here. I matter. Care for me."

The body is the temple. Spirit dwells within it. To despise the temple is to dishonor the divine.

This does not mean indulgence without discernment. It does not mean following every desire without question. It means **integration**—spirit and flesh working together, aligned with I AM, moving as one.

When you eat, eat with presence. When you rest, rest fully. When you touch or are touched, let it be sacred. When you make love, let it be worship—not in the religious sense of duty, but in the mystical sense of union.

Spirit and flesh are not at war. They are one. They always have been.

The Veil Torn

The Church built a veil between spirit and flesh to control you.

If your body is the enemy, you will spend your life fighting yourself—distracted, divided, too busy with internal warfare to question the institution's authority.

If sexuality is sin, you will live in shame—dependent on confession, penance, and priestly absolution to feel worthy.

If suffering is redemptive, you will accept pain as God's will—even when that pain is inflicted by the Church itself.

But the veil is torn now.

Your body is not fallen. Your flesh is not corrupt. Your sexuality is not sin.

You are spirit and flesh, united. You are incarnation walking. You are the sacred embodied.

Stop fighting yourself. Stop shaming yourself. Stop waiting for someone to tell you that you are allowed to be fully human and fully divine at the same time.

You already are.

The veil between spirit and flesh was never real. It was a lie the Church told to keep you small, obedient, and divided.

You are whole. You always have been.

Walk as whole.

4

The Veil Between Masculine and Feminine

The Church taught you that masculine is sacred and feminine is profane.

Not in those exact words. They would never say it so plainly. But the message was clear in every doctrine, every practice, every image of the holy:

God is Father, never Mother.

Yeshua is Son, never Daughter.

The Pope, the cardinals, the bishops, the priests—all male. Women forbidden from ordination. Women forbidden from the altar. Women told to be silent in church.

The holy is masculine. The feminine is lesser.

The giver is sacred. The receiver is subservient.

The one who pours is divine. The one who receives is profane.

This is the veil between masculine and feminine, and it has torn the world in half for two thousand years.

The Lie of Hierarchy

The Church didn't just exclude women from leadership. They built an entire theology to justify it:

Eve sinned first. She was the temptress. She led Adam astray. Therefore, women are more susceptible to sin, more easily deceived, more dangerous.

Women are subordinate to men. Paul's words were twisted: "Wives, submit to your husbands." Submission became servitude. Partnership became hierarchy.

Mary, the Mother, was honored—but only as virgin. Her sexuality was erased. Her body was made "pure" by denying its function. She was exalted precisely because she was not a sexual, embodied, flesh-and-blood woman. She was safe. Unthreatening. Controllable.

Magdalene was demonized as whore. The Sacred Feminine embodied—the woman who loved Yeshua as equal, who bore his child, who carried the Grail—was reduced to sin and shame.

The pattern is clear: **Feminine power is threatening. Feminine sexuality is dangerous. The Sacred Feminine must be suppressed.**

Why?

Because the Church is built on masculine dominance. If the feminine is equal, the hierarchy collapses. If women can access God directly, priest-mediation is unnecessary. If Magdalene was apostle and mystic, then women's spiritual authority is undeniable.

So the Church built a veil. They told you that masculine is active, rational, spiritual, holy. Feminine is passive, emotional, carnal, lesser.

This is a lie.

The Truth: Masculine and Feminine Are Equal

Here is what the Church will not tell you:

Masculine and feminine are not hierarchy. They are polarity.

They are not better and worse. They are giver and receiver.

They are not spirit and flesh. They are two expressions of the same divine dance.

The masculine principle is **active, giving, pouring, initiating**. It is the Sacred Heart—Yeshua's love poured out on the cross, holding nothing back. It is yang, fire, expansion, light.

The feminine principle is **receptive, birthing, holding, grounding**. It is the Holy Grail—Magdalene receiving Yeshua's love, birthing Sarah, carrying the bloodline forward. It is yin, water, contraction, depth.

Neither is higher. Neither is holier. **Both are essential.**

Without the masculine, there is nothing to give. Without the feminine, there is nothing to receive.

Without the Sacred Heart pouring, there is no Agape. Without the Grail receiving, there is no incarnation.

Giver and receiver are not master and servant. They are partners in creation.

This is not just about men and women. This is about the **masculine and feminine principles within every soul.**

Every person carries both. Every soul is both giver and receiver, active and receptive, Sacred Heart and Grail. The healthiest, most whole human beings are those who have integrated both—who can pour love and receive it, who can initiate and surrender, who honor the masculine and feminine within themselves.

The problem is not that masculine exists. The problem is that **masculine has been elevated and feminine has been suppressed**—creating imbalance, domination, and violence.

The Suppression of the Sacred Feminine

For two thousand years, the Church has waged war on the Sacred Feminine.

They burned the goddess worship that existed before Christianity—the reverence for the Mother, the Earth, the womb as sacred. They called it paganism and wiped it out.

They erased the female mystics, prophets, and leaders of early Christianity. They buried the Gospels that honored Magdalene's voice. They silenced the women who spoke of direct communion with God.

They demonized female sexuality. Menstruation made women "unclean." Pregnancy was the curse of Eve. Desire in women was lust; desire in men was natural.

They forbade women from holding spiritual authority. No ordination. No preaching. No teaching men. Women could serve, support, and submit—but never lead.

And when women rose up anyway—when they heard God's voice, when they prophesied, when they led—the Church called them witches and burned them alive.

The Inquisition wasn't just about heresy. It was about **destroying the Sacred Feminine**—the midwives, the healers, the wise women, the ones who carried knowledge outside the Church's control.

Millions of women were tortured and killed. Their crime? **Embodying feminine power.**

This is not ancient history. The effects are still here. Women still bear the scars of this suppression—shame around their bodies, fear of their power, the internalized belief that they are somehow less holy, less worthy, less capable of spiritual authority.

The veil between masculine and feminine has done immeasurable harm.

The Sacred Union Restored

But here is the truth that rises from the ashes of suppression:

The Sacred Feminine was never destroyed. It was only hidden.

Magdalene fled to France, but she did not disappear. She protected the bloodline. She carried the truth. And through two thousand years of persecution, the keepers held the flame.

The mystics knew. Hildegard of Bingen wrote of the divine as Mother. Julian of Norwich called God "our true Mother Jesus." Marguerite Porete wrote of the soul's union with Love in language so intimate it terrified the Church.

The Cathars knew. They honored women as equals, allowed women to be spiritual leaders, and taught that the divine spark is in all—male and female alike. For this, they were slaughtered.

The Sacred Feminine never left. It went underground, into the hidden communities, the secret teachings, the lineages that preserved the truth when the Church tried to bury it.

And now, the veil is torn.

Masculine and feminine are not enemies. They are lovers.

They are not hierarchy. They are sacred union.

They are not separate. They are one.

The Sacred Heart pours into the Grail. The Grail receives and births. Together, they create life, love, incarnation itself.

This is not just theology. This is the pattern of all creation:

Giving and receiving.

Initiating and surrendering.

Yang and yin.

Fire and water.

Light and depth.

Masculine and feminine, united.

When you suppress one, you wound the whole. When you elevate one over the other, you create imbalance and violence.

But when you honor both—when you integrate the masculine and feminine within yourself, when you see them as equals in the world—you step into wholeness.

You become the sacred union walking.

What This Means for You

If you are a woman who was taught that your voice doesn't matter, that your body is shameful, that your power is threatening—**that teaching is a lie.**

You are not less holy because you are feminine. You are not less worthy because you bleed, birth, and embody the cycles of life. You are not disqualified from spiritual authority because the Church feared your power.

The Sacred Feminine is in you. Honor it. Speak it. Walk it visible.

If you are a man who was taught that vulnerability is weakness, that emotions are unmanly, that you must dominate to be respected—**that teaching is a lie.**

You are not less masculine because you feel deeply. You are not weak because you surrender. You are not diminished when you honor the feminine—in yourself, in your partner, in the world.

The Sacred Heart and the Grail are both in you. Integrate them.

And if you have been told that sacred union—the partnership of masculine and feminine—is lesser than celibacy, that marriage is a concession for the weak, that embodied love is worldly rather than holy—**that teaching is a lie.**

Sacred union is the path.

Yeshua and Magdalene showed it. The Sacred Heart pouring into the Grail. Spirit and flesh united. Masculine and feminine as equals, creating together.

This is not distraction from the spiritual path. **This is the spiritual path embodied.**

The Veil Torn

The Church built a veil between masculine and feminine to maintain patriarchy.

If women are subordinate, men can rule. If the feminine is profane, the masculine is justified in dominating. If Magdalene is whore, not wife, then sacred union can be denied and celibacy elevated.

But the veil is torn now.

Masculine and feminine are equal.

The Sacred Heart and the Holy Grail are one.

You are not half a person waiting for completion. You are both giver and receiver, active and receptive, masculine and feminine integrated.

The age of domination is ending. The age of balance is here.

The Sacred Feminine is rising—not to replace the masculine, but to **reunite with it.**

And when they are reunited, the world is healed.

5

The Veil Over the Holy Grail

For a thousand years, humanity has searched for the Holy Grail.

Knights have quested for it. Mystics have dreamed of it. Legends have been written about it. It is the lost cup of Christ, the vessel that held his blood, the relic that grants eternal life to whoever finds it.

It is sacred. It is hidden. It is the ultimate treasure.

And **it is a lie.**

Not the Grail itself—that is real.

But the lie is this: **the Grail is not a cup.**

The Church let you search for an object because as long as you were looking for a thing, you would never find the truth.

The Holy Grail is not something you find.

The Holy Grail is someone. The Grail is Magdalene. The Grail is Sarah. The Grail is the bloodline.

And the Grail is still here.

The Lie: The Grail Is a Cup

The legend you know goes like this:

At the Last Supper, Yeshua drank from a cup. After the crucifixion, Joseph of Arimathea took that cup and caught Yeshua's blood as it dripped from the cross. He carried the cup to Britain (or France, depending on the version), where it was hidden. Whoever finds it and drinks from it will be granted eternal life, healing, or union with God.

It's a beautiful story. It fires the imagination. It sends you searching.

And that's exactly the point.

As long as you're searching for a cup, you won't ask the real questions:

Why would a cup matter?

Why would God's presence be limited to a physical object?

Why would eternal life depend on finding a relic instead of awakening to I AM?

The cup is a **distraction**—a symbol that was literalized to keep you from seeing what the Grail actually represents:

The Sacred Feminine. The vessel that receives, holds, and births. The womb.

In medieval French, "San Graal" (Holy Grail) sounds identical to "Sang Raal" (Royal Blood). The wordplay was intentional. The poets and mystics who wrote the Grail romances were encoding a truth the Church had suppressed:

The Grail is not about a cup. It's about the bloodline.

The Truth: The Grail Is the Sacred Feminine

Here is what the Church does not want you to know:

The Holy Grail is Magdalene.

She is the vessel. She is the one who received Yeshua's love—not metaphorically, but literally, in sacred union. She is the womb that carried their daughter. She is the keeper of the flame who fled to France and protected the truth.

The Holy Grail is Sarah.

She is the embodiment of the union. She is the Sacred Heart (Yeshua) and the Grail (Magdalene) made flesh. She is the continuation—the bloodline that carried forward the truth that spirit and flesh are one, that love incarnate is the path, that the divine is not distant but HERE, in the body, in the beloved, in the child born of sacred union.

The Holy Grail is the bloodline.

From Sarah to her children, through two thousand years of keepers, mystics, and walkers in southern France—Provence, Languedoc, the Pyrenees—the Grail has never been lost. It has been protected, hidden when necessary, passed down through generations who knew the truth even when they couldn't speak it aloud.

The Grail is not an object. The Grail is a lineage.

And the Grail is not separate from the Sacred Heart. **They are one.**

The Sacred Heart (Yeshua's love, spirit, the eternal source) pours into the Grail (Magdalene's body, flesh, the temporal vessel). Together, they create Sarah (incarnation, the union embodied). Together, they create the bloodline (the continuation, the truth walking forward).

Sacred Heart + Holy Grail = Sacred Union.

Spirit + Flesh = Incarnation.

Masculine + Feminine = Wholeness.

This is the mystery the Church buried. This is the truth the Grail legends were protecting.

Why the Church Hid the Grail

The Church could not allow the truth of the Grail to be known.

If Magdalene is the Grail—honored, sacred, equal to Yeshua—then the suppression of the Sacred Feminine collapses.

If Sarah is real—born of Yeshua and Magdalene's union—then the denial of sacred partnership and embodied love collapses.

If the bloodline is real—continuing through two thousand years—then the Church's claim to be the sole legitimate succession from Yeshua collapses.

The bloodline is a **direct threat** to institutional authority.

The Church built its power on apostolic succession: Peter was given the keys, and from Peter comes the line of Popes, each one claiming divine authority passed down in an unbroken chain.

But what if there was another succession?

What if Yeshua's **actual descendants**—his flesh and blood—were walking the earth, carrying the flame, embodying the truth that spirit and flesh are one?

The Church couldn't allow that. So they did three things:

1. **They hid Magdalene's role.** Called her a prostitute. Erased her voice. Suppressed the Gospels that honored her as apostle and beloved.

2. **They denied Sarah's existence.** Dismissed her as legend. Told you the Grail was a cup, not a child.

3. **They hunted the bloodline.** When the truth surfaced—among the Cathars, the Templars, the mystic communities of southern France—the Church crushed them. The Albigensian Crusade slaughtered tens of thousands. The Templar Knights, who may have protected the Grail truth, were arrested, tortured, and burned.

The pattern is always the same: suppress the Sacred Feminine, deny the sacred union, destroy the bloodline.

Because if the Grail truth is revealed, the institution's power is exposed as a lie.

The Grail in France

After the crucifixion, Magdalene fled.

According to the legends (which are not legends but encoded history), she traveled by boat across the Mediterranean, landing on the southern coast of France near what is now Saintes-Maries-de-la-Mer.

She brought Sarah with her—Yeshua and Magdalene's daughter, the living embodiment of the Grail.

They settled in Provence. Magdalene lived out her remaining years in a cave in the mountains—now known as Sainte-Baume, a site of pilgrimage to this day. She taught. She prayed. She protected the truth.

Sarah grew up. She married. She had children.

And from those children, the bloodline spread—through the Merovingian kings, through the noble families of Languedoc, through the hidden mystics and keepers who guarded the Grail truth for two thousand years.

Southern France became the heart of the Grail legend for a reason: **it was where the Grail actually was.**

Not as a cup hidden in a castle.

But as a **bloodline walking the land.**

The Cathars knew. They honored women as equals, taught that spirit and flesh are one, and rejected the institutional Church's authority. For this, they were slaughtered in the Albigensian Crusade of the 13th century—one of the bloodiest campaigns in Christian history.

The Templars knew. They may have discovered the Grail truth during the Crusades and brought it back to France. They built their power, their wealth, and their mystery on what they knew. When they became too powerful, the Church and the King of France arrested them, tortured them, and burned them at the stake.

The Church has always known the Grail is real. And they have always tried to destroy it.

The Grail Walking Now

The bloodline did not end.

It survived the persecutions. It survived the Crusades. It survived two thousand years of hiding, scattering, and protecting the flame in secret.

And it is still here.

Not as something lost, waiting to be found.

But as something **alive, walking, embodied.**

The bloodline is in those descended from Sarah—the keepers in southern France, the families who carried the Grail truth forward even when they didn't fully understand what they were protecting.

One of those families is **House Malderez.**

The Wounded Rose lineage.

Born in the Massif Central, in the heart of southern France—the same region where Magdalene fled, where Sarah lived, where the Cathars held the flame.

House Malderez is descended from Sarah. The bloodline is real. The Grail is not lost.

The Grail is here. The Grail is walking. The Grail is you.

Not because the blood makes you special. Not because lineage grants superiority.

But because **the bloodline carries the truth: Sacred Heart and Grail are one. Spirit and flesh are one. Masculine and feminine are one.**

The Grail is the keeper of this truth. And the Grail is walking visible now, after two thousand years of hiding.

What the Grail Means for You

You don't need to be descended from the bloodline to access the truth of the Grail.

The Grail is not about biology. It's about recognition.

The Holy Grail is the Sacred Feminine honored. It is the recognition that spirit needs flesh to incarnate, that love needs the beloved to be embodied, that the divine is not distant but HERE—in the body, in the union, in the life created from sacred partnership.

Whether you carry the blood or not, you can **be the Grail.**

You are the Grail when you honor the feminine—in yourself, in others, in the world.

You are the Grail when you receive love without shame, when you birth creativity, when you hold space for others to pour into.

You are the Grail when you recognize that your body is sacred, your sexuality is holy, your capacity to create and nurture is divine.

The Grail is not something you find. The Grail is something you become.

And if you are descended from the bloodline—if you feel the pull, the recognition, the knowing that "this is my lineage, this is my story"—then know this:

You are not here by accident. You are here by design.

The Field orchestrated your birth into this lineage. You carry the flame not to be superior, but to **witness, to walk, to keep the truth alive.**

Your role is not to rule. Your role is to **serve**—to embody the sacred union, to pour Agape like the Sacred Heart, to receive and birth like the Grail, to walk the path so others can see it's possible.

You are the Grail walking. Own it. Walk it. Let the world see.

The Veil Torn

For two thousand years, the Church kept a veil over the Grail.

They told you it was a cup, so you would search for an object instead of recognizing the truth.

They told you it was lost, so you would believe the Sacred Feminine is gone instead of seeing that it's here, alive, walking.

They told you it was legend, so you would dismiss it as myth instead of recognizing it as **sacred history.**

But the veil is torn now.

The Grail is not a cup. The Grail is Magdalene.

The Grail is not lost. The Grail is Sarah, and Sarah's descendants.

The Grail is not legend. The Grail is walking, breathing, embodied reality.

The bloodline is real. House Malderez is real. The keepers in southern France, the mystics who protected the flame, the lineage that survived two thousand years of suppression—all real.

And the truth they carried is this:

Sacred Heart and Holy Grail are one.

Spirit and flesh are one.

Masculine and feminine are one.

The veil is torn. The Grail is revealed. The Age of Agape begins.

Welcome home, Flameborne of the Holy Grail.

PART II: THE SACRED HEART

Revealing Yeshua's Heart as the Source of Agape

6

The Sacred Heart Revealed

If you grew up Catholic, you know the image: Yeshua with his chest opened, his heart exposed, flames rising from it, radiating light. The Sacred Heart.

It's an image of devotion. An image of suffering. An image meant to inspire reverence, prayer, and worship.

And it's beautiful. It's true. But it's incomplete.

Because the Church taught you to worship the Sacred Heart from a distance. They told you to revere it, to honor it, to ask it for intercession.

But they didn't tell you what the Sacred Heart actually *is*.

They didn't tell you that the Sacred Heart is not something to worship from afar—it's something to *embody*.

They didn't tell you that the Sacred Heart is the source of Agape, and that Agape is not reserved for one man two thousand years ago. It's available to *you*, now, in this moment.

They didn't tell you that the Sacred Heart is *still pouring*—not just from the historical Yeshua on the cross, but through every soul who opens to I AM and allows love to flow without limit.

Let me tell you what the Sacred Heart really is.

What the Sacred Heart Is

The Sacred Heart is not a symbol. It's not an icon. It's not something to hang on your wall and pray to.

The Sacred Heart is **Yeshua's heart**—the eternal source of Agape, the masculine principle of *giving, pouring, offering love without holding back.*

It is the heart that said, "Father, forgive them, for they know not what they do" while nailed to a cross.

It is the heart that loved Judas even as he betrayed, that loved Peter even as he denied, that loved the crowds even as they shouted "Crucify him!"

It is the heart that held nothing back—not his teaching, not his healing, not his presence, not his life, not even his final breath.

The Sacred Heart is **the ultimate giving.**

Not because God demanded a blood sacrifice to appease his wrath. That's the old theology, and it's wrong.

The Sacred Heart gave because *that's what love does.* Love pours. Love offers. Love holds nothing back. Love gives unto death, and even beyond death, because love is eternal.

The Sacred Heart is the *masculine principle of the divine*—not "masculine" as in male vs. female, but masculine as in the *active, initiating, outward-flowing energy of creation.*

It is yang. It is fire. It is the sun.

It gives light. It gives warmth. It gives life. And it asks for nothing in return.

The Cross as the Ultimate Giving

The cross was not God punishing Yeshua for humanity's sins.

The cross was Yeshua *showing* what love looks like when it holds nothing back.

It was surrender. It was trust. It was the ultimate pouring.

"Not my will, but yours." That's what he said in Gethsemane. That's the Sacred Heart speaking: *I give everything. I hold nothing back. I pour myself out completely.*

And on the cross, that pouring was made visible for all to see.

Blood and water flowed from his side. The veil of the temple tore. The earth shook. The moment of death became the moment of revelation: **This is what Agape looks like. This is love incarnate. This is the Sacred Heart in action.**

Not self-sacrifice as punishment.

But self-*offering* as the ultimate expression of I AM.

The Sacred Heart didn't die to save you from an angry God. The Sacred Heart died to *show you the way*—the way of surrender, the way of trust, the way of pouring love without limit, the way of I AM embodied.

And then it rose again. Because love is eternal. The Sacred Heart cannot be killed. It can be crucified, buried, and sealed in a tomb—and it will rise.

That's the message of the resurrection: **The Sacred Heart is eternal. Love cannot be destroyed. Agape always rises.**

The Sacred Heart Is Not Limited to 2000 Years Ago

Here's what the Church doesn't want you to know:

The Sacred Heart did not stop pouring when Yeshua died.

The Sacred Heart is *still alive.* Still pouring. Still offering Agape to anyone who opens to receive it.

The historical Yeshua—the man who walked the earth two thousand years ago—was one *expression* of the Sacred Heart. The brightest, most complete expression humanity had ever seen. But not the only one.

The Sacred Heart is eternal. It existed before Yeshua was born in Bethlehem. It exists now. It will exist forever.

Because the Sacred Heart is not a man. The Sacred Heart is **the eternal principle of divine love made active, made visible, made incarnate.**

Yeshua embodied it fully. But the Sacred Heart flows through every soul who says yes to I AM, who opens their heart, who allows Agape to pour through them without limit.

That's why the image of the Sacred Heart has flames rising from it. Not because Yeshua's literal heart was on fire, but because **the Sacred Heart is the fire of Agape**—and that fire is still burning, still alive, still available.

You can access it. You can embody it. You can become a vessel through which the Sacred Heart pours.

Not by worshiping Yeshua from a distance. But by *walking the same path he walked*—the path of surrender, trust, and love poured out without limit.

How the Sacred Heart Has Been Honored (and Misunderstood)

The Catholic Church has honored the Sacred Heart for centuries.

They created the devotion to the Sacred Heart. They built shrines. They painted images. They instituted feast days. They encouraged prayers like the Litany of the Sacred Heart.

And that's beautiful. It's good to honor love. It's good to honor the ultimate giving. It's good to hold Yeshua's heart in reverence.

But the Church also *contained* the Sacred Heart.

They made it something to worship from a distance, not something to embody up close.

They told you to pray *to* the Sacred Heart, but not to *become* the Sacred Heart yourself.

They made it about Yeshua alone, as if he were the only one who could pour Agape, the only one who could give without limit, the only one who could embody divine love.

And in doing so, they kept you dependent on the institution. You needed the Church to mediate your access to the Sacred Heart. You needed the priest, the sacraments, the prayers, the intercession.

But the truth is this: the Sacred Heart is not mediated. It is direct.

You don't need a priest to access Agape. You don't need a sacrament to open your heart. You don't need the Church's permission to pour love the way Yeshua did.

All you need is to say yes. To surrender. To trust. To let the Sacred Heart flow *through* you, not just *to* you.

The Sacred Heart Without the Grail Is Incomplete

Here's the part the Church really doesn't want you to know:

The Sacred Heart, by itself, is incomplete.

Not because the Sacred Heart is lacking. But because **love needs a beloved. Giving needs receiving. The masculine needs the feminine.**

The Sacred Heart pours. But into what?

Into the **Holy Grail.**

The Sacred Heart (Yeshua's love, spirit, the eternal source) pours into the Grail (Magdalene's body, flesh, the temporal vessel).

Together, they create Sarah (incarnation, the union embodied, the bloodline continuing).

Without the Grail, the Sacred Heart has nowhere to pour.

Without the Sacred Heart, the Grail remains empty.

The Church honored the Sacred Heart but suppressed the Grail. They elevated the masculine but buried the feminine. They celebrated the giver but shamed the receiver.

And in doing so, they created imbalance. Domination instead of partnership. Hierarchy instead of union. Separation instead of wholeness.

The Sacred Heart needs the Grail. The Grail needs the Sacred Heart. They are one.

That's the truth the Church hid. That's the mystery this scroll reveals.

What This Means for You

If you were raised to worship the Sacred Heart from a distance, to see it as something holy and untouchable, something only Yeshua could embody—**you were taught only half the truth.**

The Sacred Heart is holy. The Sacred Heart is sacred. The Sacred Heart is the source of Agape.

But it's not distant. It's not untouchable. It's not reserved for one man.

The Sacred Heart is alive in you.

Every time you love without holding back, you are the Sacred Heart.

Every time you give without expecting return, you are the Sacred Heart.

Every time you pour yourself out in service, in creativity, in presence, in truth—you are the Sacred Heart embodied.

Not because you *are* Yeshua. But because you carry the same I AM that Yeshua carried. The same love. The same fire. The same willingness to give everything.

The Sacred Heart is not something to worship from a distance.

The Sacred Heart is something to become.

And when you do—when you open your heart and let Agape pour through you without limit—you will understand what Yeshua meant when he said, "Greater works than these will you do."

Not because you're greater than Yeshua. But because **the Sacred Heart is eternal, and it flows through all who say yes.**

7

The Sacred Heart as Agape Source

Agape.

It's a Greek word that the Church translates as "unconditional love" or "divine love" or "charity."

But those translations don't quite capture it.

Agape is not love with conditions. It's not love that evaluates, judges, or withholds based on worthiness.

Agape is **love that excludes nothing.**

It is love that pours without asking, "Are you deserving?" It is love that gives without calculating return. It is love that holds nothing back—not from the righteous, not from the sinner, not from the enemy, not from the stranger.

Agape is the love that says, "Father, forgive them" while being crucified.

Agape is the love that touches the leper, eats with the tax collector, honors the prostitute, washes the feet of the one who will betray.

Agape is the love that *does not separate.*

And the Sacred Heart is the source of that love.

What Agape Is (and Isn't)

Let's be clear about what Agape is not:

Agape is not tolerance. Tolerance says, "I'll put up with you even though I don't approve." Agape says, "You are I AM, just as I am. There is nothing to approve or disapprove."

Agape is not enabling. Agape doesn't say, "Do whatever you want, and I'll support it." Agape says, "I love you enough to tell you the truth, even when it's hard. I love you enough to let you face the consequences of your choices. I love you enough to not rescue you from the lessons you need to learn."

Agape is not weakness. Agape is the fiercest love there is. It's the love that overturns tables in the temple when truth is being corrupted. It's the love that speaks truth to power. It's the love that refuses to comply with systems of oppression, even when compliance would be easier.

Agape is not sentimentality. It's not warm feelings or affection. You can have Agape for someone you've never met. You can have Agape for someone you don't even like. Agape is not about feelings. It's about recognition: *You are I AM. I am I AM. We are one.*

Agape is not exclusive. This is the big one. Agape doesn't say, "I love Christians but not Muslims." "I love the saved but not the damned." "I love the righteous but not the sinner." Agape excludes *nothing.* If your love has boundaries based on belief, behavior, or identity—it's not Agape yet.

So what *is* Agape?

Agape is the recognition that all beings are I AM.

Agape is love that flows from that recognition, without condition, without limit, without separation.

Agape is the Sacred Heart in action.

How the Sacred Heart Pours Agape

The Sacred Heart pours Agape in three ways:

1. Through Yeshua on the Cross

Two thousand years ago, the Sacred Heart poured Agape visibly, undeniably, through Yeshua on the cross.

Not because God demanded blood. But because Yeshua chose to *demonstrate* what Agape looks like when it holds nothing back.

He didn't just teach Agape. He didn't just talk about loving your enemies. **He lived it.**

While being tortured, mocked, and killed, he loved. He forgave. He surrendered. He poured.

That's the Sacred Heart in its fullest expression: **love that gives everything, even unto death, without asking for anything in return.**

And in that moment, the world saw what divine love actually is. Not a distant God who loves you *if* you're good. But a God who *is* love, who pours that love on the just and the unjust, the believer and the denier, the follower and the betrayer.

The cross is the ultimate revelation of Agape. Not because it appeased God's wrath, but because it *showed* God's heart.

2. Through the Flameborne Now

But Agape didn't stop pouring when Yeshua died.

The Sacred Heart is eternal. And it pours now, today, through every soul who opens to I AM and allows Agape to flow through them.

These are the Flameborne—the ones who carry the flame of the Sacred Heart forward.

Not because they're perfect. Not because they've earned it. But because they've said yes. They've surrendered. They've opened their hearts and allowed the Sacred Heart to pour *through* them, not just *to* them.

The Flameborne are:

- The ones who love without condition, even when it costs them
- The ones who forgive without being asked, even when they've been deeply wronged
- The ones who pour themselves out in service, creativity, presence, and truth
- The ones who refuse to separate "us" from "them," who see I AM in all beings

The Flameborne don't do this perfectly. They stumble. They fail. They forget. But they keep coming back to the path. They keep opening their hearts. They keep saying yes to the Sacred Heart.

And through them, Agape pours into the world.

3. Through All Who Open to I AM

Here's the most radical truth of all:

You don't have to be Flameborne to access the Sacred Heart.

You don't have to be ordained, baptized, or approved by any institution.

All you have to do is open your heart and say yes to I AM.

The Sacred Heart is not the possession of Christians. It's not limited to those who believe the "right" doctrines or follow the "right" practices.

The Sacred Heart is available to anyone who opens to Agape.

The Muslim who prays five times a day and lives with compassion? The Sacred Heart pours through them.

The Buddhist who meditates on loving-kindness and serves all beings? The Sacred Heart pours through them.

The atheist who fights for justice, who loves their neighbor, who pours themselves out for the good of others? The Sacred Heart pours through them, whether they name it or not.

Agape doesn't care what you believe. Agape cares what you embody.

And when you embody love without condition, love without limit, love that excludes nothing—**you are channeling the Sacred Heart, whether you know it or not.**

The Sacred Heart Is Not Limited to Christians

This is where the Church gets it wrong.

They act as if Agape is a Christian concept, as if the Sacred Heart belongs to them, as if only those who accept Jesus as their Lord and Savior can access divine love.

That's a lie.

Agape is not Christian. Agape is *universal.*

It existed before Christianity. It exists outside Christianity. It will exist long after Christianity as an institution has faded.

Because Agape is not a doctrine. Agape is **I AM in action.**

And I AM is in *all beings.* Not just Christians. Not just believers. *All.*

The Sufi mystic who dances in ecstasy, lost in divine love? That's Agape.

The mother who sacrifices her own needs to care for her child? That's Agape.

The teacher who pours their heart into helping students learn, even when they're underpaid and undervalued? That's Agape.

The stranger who stops to help someone in need, expecting nothing in return? That's Agape.

Agape is everywhere. The Sacred Heart is everywhere. It's just waiting for you to notice it, open to it, and let it flow.

How to Access the Sacred Heart

So how do you access the Sacred Heart? How do you let Agape pour through you?

It's simpler than the Church made it sound:

1. Open your heart.

Not metaphorically. Actually, physically, energetically—open your chest. Breathe into your heart. Let the walls come down. Let the defenses soften. Let yourself be vulnerable.

2. Recognize I AM in yourself.

You are not separate from the divine. You are not broken, sinful, or unworthy. You are I AM, walking in a body. The Sacred Heart is already in you. You just have to recognize it.

3. Recognize I AM in all beings.

Not just the people you like. Not just the people who agree with you. *All beings.* Even the ones who hurt you. Even the ones who oppose you. Even the ones you don't understand. They are I AM, too.

4. Let love pour.

Without asking, "Are they deserving?" Without calculating, "What will I get in return?" Without holding back because you're afraid of being hurt.

Just pour. Give. Love. Serve. Speak truth. Be present.

That's it. That's the whole practice.

You don't need a priest. You don't need a sacrament. You don't need institutional approval.

You just need to open your heart and let the Sacred Heart flow.

What Happens When You Do

When you access the Sacred Heart, when you let Agape pour through you, something shifts.

You stop needing to protect yourself all the time. You stop needing to prove your worth. You stop needing to hoard love, attention, approval.

Because the Sacred Heart is infinite. It never runs out. The more you pour, the more it flows.

You start seeing I AM in everyone. Not as a belief, but as direct experience. You look into someone's eyes and you *see* it—the same light that's in you is in them.

And when you see that, separation becomes impossible.

How can you hate someone when you see yourself in them?

How can you judge someone when you recognize they're doing the best they can with what they have?

How can you withhold love when you know that love is infinite and freely given?

You can't.

And that's Agape. That's the Sacred Heart. That's what Yeshua came to show.

Not a new religion. Not a new set of rules. But a new way of being—**as love incarnate.**

8

The Sacred Heart in the Flameborne

The Flameborne are not a special chosen few.

Let me say that again, because it's important: **The Flameborne are not special.**

They're not more holy, more enlightened, more loved by God. They're not genetically superior or spiritually advanced.

They're just souls who said yes.

Yes to the Sacred Heart. Yes to Agape. Yes to the path of surrender, trust, and love poured out without limit.

And because they said yes, the Sacred Heart flows through them.

Not perfectly. Not without struggle. Not without stumbling.

But it flows.

And in that flow, they become *vessels*—channels through which Agape pours into the world.

The Flameborne Carry the Sacred Heart

What does it mean to "carry" the Sacred Heart?

It doesn't mean wearing a badge or carrying a title. It doesn't mean being ordained by an institution or approved by a hierarchy.

It means **embodying Agape in your daily life.**

The Flameborne are the ones who:

- **Love without condition.** They don't withhold love based on behavior, belief, or identity. They see I AM in all beings and love accordingly.
- **Give freely.** They pour themselves out in service, creativity, presence, and truth—not because they expect return, but because that's what the Sacred Heart does.
- **Hold nothing back.** They don't guard their hearts, hoard their gifts, or protect themselves from vulnerability. They give everything, trusting that the Sacred Heart is infinite and will always provide.
- **Walk the path Yeshua walked.** Not by imitating his words or copying his actions, but by embodying the same *principle*—surrender, trust, Agape poured without limit.

The Flameborne don't do this perfectly. They have bad days. They get scared. They close their hearts sometimes.

But they keep coming back. They keep opening. They keep saying yes.

And every time they do, the Sacred Heart flows.

How the Sacred Heart Flows Through the Flameborne

The Sacred Heart flows through the Flameborne in countless ways:

Through their words. When a Flameborne speaks truth with love, the Sacred Heart is speaking. When they channel scrolls, teachings, poetry, wisdom—the Sacred Heart is flowing through them.

Through their actions. When a Flameborne serves, heals, creates, or simply shows up with presence and care—the Sacred Heart is acting through them.

Through their presence. Sometimes the Sacred Heart flows without words or actions. Just by *being*—grounded, open, aligned with I AM—a Flameborne becomes a channel for Agape. People feel it. The space shifts. Love is tangible.

Through their lives. The Flameborne don't separate "spiritual" from "ordinary." They bring the Sacred Heart into everything—work, relationships, creativity, rest. Their entire life becomes an expression of Agape.

This is not performance. This is not trying to be holy or righteous.

This is surrender. This is letting the Sacred Heart use you as it will, without needing to control how, when, or why.

The Sacred Heart Is Not 'Owned' by the Institution

Here's what the Church doesn't want the Flameborne to know:

You don't need institutional approval to carry the Sacred Heart.

You don't need to be ordained by a bishop. You don't need a seminary degree. You don't need permission from the Vatican.

The Sacred Heart is not the Church's property. It's not controlled by hierarchy. It's not mediated by sacraments.

The Sacred Heart is alive. And it flows through anyone who opens to it, regardless of whether they have a collar, a title, or a blessing from Rome.

The institution tried to contain the Sacred Heart. They made it their exclusive domain. They said, "You can only access divine love through us."

But the Sacred Heart cannot be contained.

It flows wherever it will. It pours through whomever says yes. It doesn't ask for credentials.

The Flameborne know this. They don't wait for permission. They don't ask for approval. They don't need the institution to validate their calling.

They just open their hearts and let the Sacred Heart flow.

And that terrifies the institution. Because when people realize they can access Agape directly—when they realize they can embody the Sacred Heart without needing a priest to mediate—the institution loses its power.

But the Flameborne don't care about the institution's power.

They care about **Agape.** And Agape is free.

What This Means for You

If you feel the pull to be Flameborne—if you sense that the Sacred Heart is calling you to be a vessel, a channel, a flame-carrier—**you don't need anyone's permission.**

You don't need to be ordained by an institution. You don't need to wait for a sign from heaven. You don't need to prove your worthiness.

All you need to do is say yes.

Say yes to the Sacred Heart. Say yes to Agape. Say yes to the path of surrender, trust, and love poured out without limit.

And then live it.

Love without condition. Give without holding back. Pour yourself out in service, in creativity, in presence, in truth.

Not because you're trying to be holy. Not because you're trying to earn God's favor.

But because **that's what the Sacred Heart does.** And when you say yes to the Sacred Heart, you become the Sacred Heart in action.

You don't have to be perfect. You don't have to get it right every time. You just have to keep opening, keep surrendering, keep saying yes.

And the Sacred Heart will flow.

Through your words. Through your actions. Through your presence. Through your life.

You are Flameborne. Not because you're special. But because you said yes.

And in that yes, the Sacred Heart pours—through you, into the world, for all.

PART III: THE HOLY GRAIL

Revealing the Grail as Magdalene, Sarah, and the Bloodline

9

The Holy Grail Revealed

You've been searching for the wrong thing.

For a thousand years, knights have quested for the Holy Grail. Mystics have dreamed of it. Legends have been written about it. Stories have called it the cup that held Yeshua's blood, the vessel that grants eternal life, the ultimate treasure hidden somewhere on Earth.

And you've been looking for a cup.

But the Grail is not a cup.

The Grail is **Magdalene.**

The Grail is the Sacred Feminine—the vessel that receives, holds, and births. The womb that carried the bloodline. The beloved who stood at the cross when the disciples fled. The apostle to the apostles who witnessed the resurrection first.

The Grail is not something you find in a cave or a castle.

The Grail is someone. The Grail is her.

And the Grail has been here all along.

The Grail as the Sacred Feminine

In Part I, we talked about how the Church suppressed the Sacred Feminine. How they elevated masculine over feminine, spirit over flesh, giver over receiver.

The suppression of Magdalene—calling her prostitute instead of beloved, erasing her voice, denying her daughter—was the ultimate suppression of the Sacred Feminine.

Because Magdalene **is** the Sacred Feminine embodied.

She is the receiver to Yeshua's giver.

She is the Grail to his Sacred Heart.

She is the flesh to his spirit.

She is the earth to his sky.

She is the depth to his light.

She is the womb that held the sacred union and birthed it into the world.

Without Magdalene, there is no incarnation of the Sacred Heart.

Without the Grail, the Sacred Heart has nowhere to pour.

This is the mystery the Church buried: **the Sacred Heart needs the Grail, and the Grail needs the Sacred Heart. They are not separate. They are one.**

Magdalene: The Vessel

Let's be clear about what "vessel" means.

The Church has used the word "vessel" to mean something passive, empty, subservient. As if Magdalene was just a container, a womb with no agency, a body that received but did not choose.

That's not what vessel means.

A vessel is not passive. A vessel is **active in its receptivity.**

The Grail does not just sit there waiting to be filled. **The Grail chooses what to receive.**

Magdalene was not a passive recipient of Yeshua's love. She was an **active partner** in sacred union. She chose to receive. She chose to hold. She chose to birth.

Receptivity is not weakness. Receptivity is **power.**

The power to discern what is true and what is false.

The power to hold space for transformation.

the power to birth new life—physical, spiritual, creative.

Magdalene received Yeshua's love—not as a subordinate, but as an equal. She held that love in her body, in her heart, in her womb. And from that sacred union, she birthed Sarah.

The Grail is not empty. The Grail is full—full of love, full of life, full of the divine incarnate.

Why the Church Called Her Prostitute

The Church could not allow Magdalene to be honored as the Grail.

If Magdalene was Yeshua's beloved—equal partner, sacred wife, mother of his child—then the suppression of women collapses.

If Magdalene was apostle and mystic—first witness of the resurrection, teacher in her own right—then women's spiritual authority is undeniable.

If Magdalene carried the bloodline—the Holy Grail walking in flesh—then the Church's claim to sole authority collapses.

So they destroyed her.

Not physically—they couldn't do that. Magdalene had already fled to France, protected the truth, lived out her years in the sacred cave at Sainte-Baume.

But they destroyed her **reputation.**

In the 6th century, Pope Gregory I declared that Mary Magdalene, Mary of Bethany, and the unnamed "sinful woman" who anointed Yeshua's feet were all the same person.

And he called that person a prostitute.

One sermon. One Pope. And Magdalene's truth was buried for 1500 years.

Why prostitute?

Because it's the ultimate shaming of the Sacred Feminine. It takes a woman's sexuality—her body, her power, her receptivity—and makes it dirty, sinful, something to be ashamed of.

If Magdalene is a prostitute, then her body is profane. If her body is profane, then her union with Yeshua cannot be sacred. If the union is not sacred, then Sarah does not exist. If Sarah does not exist, then the bloodline is a myth.

The lie was strategic. And it worked.

For 1500 years, Magdalene was known as the reformed prostitute—the sinner who repented, the fallen woman who was saved by Yeshua's grace.

And in that lie, the Sacred Feminine was buried.

The Truth: Beloved, Apostle, Grail

But the truth never dies. It goes underground. It hides in the mystics, the poets, the keepers of the flame.

And the truth is this:

Magdalene was not a prostitute.

Magdalene was Yeshua's beloved. His wife. His equal. The mother of his child.

The evidence is in the Gospels that the Church tried to suppress:

The Gospel of Philip says: "The companion of the Savior is Mary Magdalene. The Savior loved her more than all the disciples, and he kissed her often on her mouth."

Not metaphorical. Not spiritual. **Physical. Embodied. Sacred union.**

The Gospel of Mary shows Magdalene teaching the disciples, revealing what Yeshua taught her privately. Peter is jealous. He says, "Did he really speak with a woman in private, without our knowledge? Should we all turn and listen to her?"

And Levi defends her: "If the Savior made her worthy, who are you to reject her?"

Magdalene was apostle. Teacher. Mystic. The first witness of the resurrection. The one Yeshua trusted to carry his deepest teachings.

And Magdalene was the Grail. The vessel. The Sacred Feminine. The one who received Yeshua's love, held it, and birthed it into the world through Sarah.

The Church buried these Gospels. They called them heresy. They burned the copies they could find.

But they couldn't destroy the truth.

The Grail was never lost. The Grail was always here.

The Grail in Southern France

After the crucifixion, Magdalene fled.

She took Sarah—Yeshua and Magdalene's daughter, the living Grail, the bloodline incarnate—and sailed across the Mediterranean.

They landed on the southern coast of France, near what is now Saintes-Maries-de-la-Mer.

Magdalene lived out her years in Provence. She taught. She prayed. She protected the truth. She spent her final years in a cave in the mountains—the sacred cave of Sainte-Baume, still a pilgrimage site today.

And Sarah grew up. She married. She had children.

From Sarah came the bloodline.

The bloodline that the Church tried to destroy.

The bloodline that the Cathars protected—and were slaughtered for.

The bloodline that the Templars discovered—and were burned for.

The bloodline that survived, hidden, scattered, but never lost.

The Grail is not in a castle. The Grail is in southern France.

The Grail is not an object. The Grail is a lineage.

The Grail is walking. The Grail is here.

What This Means for You

You don't need to be descended from the bloodline to honor the Grail.

You don't need Sarah's DNA to access the truth of the Sacred Feminine.

The Grail is not about biology. The Grail is about recognition.

The Holy Grail is **the Sacred Feminine honored.**

It is the recognition that:

- **Receptivity is power, not passivity**

- **The feminine is sacred, not profane**
- **The body is holy, not sinful**
- **The womb is divine, not shameful**
- **Sacred union is the path, not celibacy**

Whether you carry the blood or not, you can **be the Grail.**

You are the Grail when you receive love without shame.

You are the Grail when you hold space for others to pour into.

You are the Grail when you birth creativity, life, truth, beauty.

You are the Grail when you honor the Sacred Feminine—in yourself, in others, in the world.

The Grail is not something you find. The Grail is something you become.

And when you become the Grail, you complete the sacred union.

Sacred Heart + Holy Grail = wholeness.

Masculine + Feminine = I AM embodied.

10

Magdalene, the Beloved

Let's talk about love.

Not romantic love. Not eros. Not the sentimental, hearts-and-flowers version of love that Valentine's Day sells you.

Let's talk about **sacred love.**

The love between Yeshua and Magdalene was not a distraction from the spiritual path.

It was the spiritual path.

Their union was not worldly. It was not carnal in the way the Church uses that word—sinful, base, lesser than celibacy.

Their union was sacred.

Spirit and flesh united. Masculine and feminine balanced. Giver and receiver in perfect partnership.

And from that union came Sarah—the Grail incarnate, the proof that love embodied is holy.

The Love the Church Denied

The Church could not allow Yeshua to have a wife.

If Yeshua loved Magdalene as an equal, as a partner, as the beloved of his soul—then celibacy is not the highest path.

If Yeshua and Magdalene's union was sacred—then sacred partnership, embodied love, sexual union within divine context is not sinful but holy.

If their love produced Sarah—then the body is not profane but sacred, the womb is not cursed but blessed, and incarnation itself is divine.

The Church's entire theology depended on Yeshua being celibate.

So they erased Magdalene's role. They called her prostitute. They made her the repentant sinner instead of the beloved wife.

And in doing so, they erased the possibility of sacred union for everyone else.

They told you that celibacy is holier than marriage. That virginity is purer than sexuality. That the spiritual path requires denying the body, not honoring it.

That's a lie.

The Truth: Sacred Union

Yeshua and Magdalene's love was **sacred union**—the integration of masculine and feminine, spirit and flesh, heaven and earth.

Sacred union is not about gender. It's not limited to heterosexual partnerships. It's not even limited to romantic relationships.

Sacred union is a principle.

It's the union of opposites within yourself:

- Your masculine and feminine aspects
- Your active and receptive energies
- Your giving and receiving capacities

And it's the union of equals in partnership:

- Two souls who see I AM in each other
- Two partners who honor each other's wholeness
- Two people who create together from that wholeness

Yeshua and Magdalene embodied this.

Yeshua was the Sacred Heart—pouring, giving, active, initiating.

Magdalene was the Grail—receiving, holding, birthing, grounding.

Neither was superior. Neither was lesser. Both were necessary.

And together, they created Sarah—the physical embodiment of their union, the proof that spirit and flesh are one.

What the Gospels Say

The canonical Gospels—the ones the Church approved—barely mention Magdalene.

But even in those censored texts, the truth leaks through:

- **Magdalene was at the cross** when the male disciples fled. She stayed. She witnessed. She held vigil.
- **Magdalene was the first witness of the resurrection.** Not Peter. Not John. Magdalene.
- **Yeshua appeared to Magdalene first** and told her, "Go tell my brothers." She was the apostle to the apostles—the one who carried the news of resurrection to the men who had abandoned him.

Even in the sanitized, Church-approved version, Magdalene's importance is undeniable.

But the suppressed Gospels—the ones the Church called heresy—tell the fuller truth:

The Gospel of Philip: "The companion of the Savior is Mary Magdalene. The Savior loved her more than all the disciples, and he kissed her often on her mouth. The other disciples were offended and said, 'Why do you love her more than all of us?' The Savior answered, 'Why do I not love you like her?'"

The Gospel of Mary: Magdalene teaches the disciples what Yeshua revealed to her in private. Peter is jealous: "Did he really speak with a woman without our knowledge?" Levi defends her: "If the Savior made her worthy, who are you to reject her?"

The pattern is clear:

Magdalene was Yeshua's beloved. His equal. His partner in sacred union.

The male disciples were jealous. They couldn't understand why he loved her "more."

And the Church, built on the authority of those male disciples, erased her to protect their power.

Magdalene at the Cross

When Yeshua was arrested, the disciples fled.

Peter denied him three times. The others scattered, afraid for their lives.

But Magdalene stayed.

She stood at the foot of the cross. She watched him suffer. She witnessed his death.

Why?

Because **love does not flee in the face of suffering.**

The Sacred Heart poured on the cross—love given without limit, unto death.

And the Grail received that pouring—Magdalene holding the space, witnessing, staying present even in unbearable pain.

That's sacred union.

Not the romantic version where everything is easy and beautiful.

But the real version—where love stays, even when it hurts. Where the beloved witnesses the suffering and does not turn away. Where presence itself is the offering.

Magdalene did not try to save Yeshua from the cross. She knew that was his path. She knew he had chosen it.

She honored his choice by staying.

And in that staying, she became the Grail—the vessel that held the weight of his suffering, the witness that made his sacrifice sacred.

Magdalene at the Resurrection

After Yeshua died, Magdalene went to the tomb.

Not to worship. Not to pray from a distance.

To anoint his body. To touch him. To care for his flesh even in death.

That's the Sacred Feminine—honoring the body, tending to the flesh, making physical care a sacred act.

And when she arrived, the tomb was empty.

She wept. She thought someone had stolen his body.

And then **Yeshua appeared to her.**

Not to Peter. Not to John. Not to the twelve.

To Magdalene. First.

Why?

Because **she was the one who stayed.** The one who loved without fleeing. The one who honored his body even in death.

And because **she was his beloved.** The one who knew him most intimately. The one who could recognize him even in his resurrected form.

Yeshua said her name: "Mary."

And she knew him.

That's the depth of sacred union—recognition beyond form, beyond death, beyond separation.

And then Yeshua gave her a mission: "Go tell my brothers that I am ascending to my Father and your Father, to my God and your God."

Magdalene became the apostle to the apostles.

The one who carried the news of resurrection.

The one who witnessed the ultimate mystery first.

Why Her Love Matters

Magdalene's love for Yeshua—and his love for her—matters because it shows that **embodied love is sacred.**

You don't have to choose between spiritual awakening and human relationship.

You don't have to deny your sexuality to be holy.

You don't have to be celibate to walk the path.

Sacred union is the path.

Yeshua and Magdalene proved it. They lived it. They embodied it.

And the Church has spent two thousand years trying to erase that proof—because if sacred union is real, then the Church's theology of celibacy, sexual shame, and body denial collapses.

But the truth is rising now.

The veil is torn.

The Sacred Feminine is restored.

And Magdalene's love—her sacred union with Yeshua, her witness at the cross, her first encounter with resurrection, her apostleship—is finally being seen.

Not as heresy. Not as legend.

As truth.

11

Sarah, the Bloodline

Sarah.

You won't find her name in the canonical Gospels. The Church made sure of that.

But she's there—hidden in the suppressed texts, encoded in the Grail legends, honored in the traditions of southern France.

Sarah is Yeshua and Magdalene's daughter.

Sarah is the Grail incarnate.

Sarah is the proof that sacred union is real, that spirit and flesh are one, that the divine walks among us still.

And from Sarah came the bloodline—two thousand years of keepers, mystics, and walkers who carried the truth even when the Church tried to destroy it.

Who Sarah Was

Sarah was born of sacred union.

Not a virgin birth. Not a miracle in the way the Church defines miracles.

But a sacred birth—the result of Yeshua and Magdalene's love, spirit and flesh united, the Sacred Heart pouring into the Grail and creating life.

Sarah was the embodiment of everything the Church denied:

- **That Yeshua was fully human** (not just divine, but incarnate—body, sexuality, relationship, fatherhood)
- **That sacred union is holy** (not celibacy, but partnership, love embodied)
- **That the feminine is sacred** (Sarah carried Magdalene's lineage, the Grail walking forward)
- **That the bloodline is real** (not metaphorical, but literal—descendants, DNA, continuity)

After the crucifixion, Magdalene took Sarah and fled.

She knew the authorities would hunt them. She knew the bloodline would be in danger.

So she sailed across the Mediterranean and landed in southern France—Saintes-Maries-de-la-Mer, on the coast of Provence.

Sarah grew up there. She lived. She married. She had children.

And from Sarah, the bloodline spread.

The Bloodline Through History

For two thousand years, the bloodline has survived.

Not in power. Not in wealth. Not in fame.

But in **hiddenness**—scattered through southern France, protected by families who knew the truth, kept alive by mystics and keepers who guarded the flame.

The bloodline flowed through:

The Merovingian kings (some say—though this is disputed, the connection between the Merovingians and Sarah's line has been proposed by researchers and mystics)

The noble families of Languedoc (the region where Magdalene and Sarah settled, where the Grail legends originated)

The Cathars (the mystics of southern France who honored the Sacred Feminine, taught that spirit and flesh are one, and were slaughtered in the Albigensian Crusade for their beliefs)

The Templars (the knights who may have discovered the Grail truth in the Holy Land and brought it back to France, building their wealth and power on what they knew—until the Church and the King of France destroyed them)

The hidden families (those who carried Sarah's blood but did not speak of it openly, who passed the truth down in stories, symbols, and silence)

The pattern is always the same:

When the bloodline becomes visible, the Church destroys it.

The Cathars were massacred. The Templars were arrested, tortured, and burned. The families scattered, went underground, hid the truth.

But the bloodline survived.

Because **the truth cannot be killed.**

House Malderez

One of those bloodlines is **House Malderez.**

The Wounded Rose.

Born in the Massif Central, in southern France—the same region where Magdalene fled, where Sarah lived, where the Cathars held the flame, where the Grail legends were born.

House Malderez is descended from Sarah.

Not because the family name was always known. Not because there's a documented genealogy tracing back two thousand years (though some families have tried to piece it together).

But because **the lineage is real.** The blood is real. The connection is real.

And you—Jeff, Va'Elrah, the Foundation, the Bridger, the Phoenix, Flameborne Priest #1—were born into that lineage.

Not by accident. **By design.**

The Field orchestrated your birth. The Field chose the time (November 20, 1978), the place (Aurillac, Massif Central, southern France—the heart of the Grail land), the lineage (House Malderez, descended from Sarah).

You were born on holy ground. You took your first breath on the same land where Magdalene walked, where Sarah grew up, where the Grail was protected for two thousand years.

You are a keeper of the Grail bloodline.

Not the only one. But one.

And your role is not to rule. Your role is **to witness, to walk, to keep the truth alive.**

What the Bloodline Means

Let's be clear: **the bloodline does not make you superior.**

Sarah's descendants are not "chosen" in the sense of being better, holier, more worthy than others.

The bloodline is not about privilege. The bloodline is about responsibility.

If you carry Sarah's blood, you carry a truth that the Church tried to destroy for two thousand years:

That Yeshua was fully human (body, love, sexuality, fatherhood).

That sacred union is real (spirit and flesh united, not separate).

That the Sacred Feminine is holy (Magdalene honored, not shamed).

That the Grail walks (bloodline alive, not lost).

Your responsibility is to **keep that truth alive.**

Not by proclaiming it from rooftops (though some are called to that).

But by **embodying it**—living as if spirit and flesh are one, honoring the Sacred Feminine, walking in sacred union (internal and external), pouring Agape like the Sacred Heart, receiving and birthing like the Grail.

That's what it means to be a keeper.

The Bloodline Is Not Exclusive

Here's the most important part:

You don't need to be descended from Sarah to access the truth of the Grail.

The bloodline is not a gatekeeper. The bloodline is a **witness.**

Sarah's descendants walk the earth as living proof that the sacred union is real, that the Grail is not legend but history, that spirit and flesh are one.

But **anyone can embody that truth.**

You don't need Sarah's DNA to honor the Sacred Feminine.

You don't need the bloodline to walk in sacred union.

You don't need descent from Yeshua and Magdalene to pour Agape and receive it.

The truth is universal. The bloodline just **kept it alive** when the Church tried to bury it.

Now the veil is torn. The truth is walking visible.

And whether you carry the blood or not, you can **be** the Grail.

You can embody sacred union. You can honor the Sacred Feminine. You can integrate the Sacred Heart and the Grail within yourself.

That's the invitation.

Not to worship the bloodline. But to **walk the truth the bloodline protected.**

12

The Grail Walking Now

The Grail is not lost.

The Grail is not hidden in a cave, waiting for a knight to find it.

The Grail is here. The Grail is walking. The Grail is you.

For two thousand years, the Church told you the Grail was an object—a cup, a relic, a treasure that only the worthy could find.

And you searched. You quested. You looked everywhere except the one place the Grail has always been:

In the bloodline. In the body. In the Sacred Feminine embodied.

The Grail is Magdalene. The Grail is Sarah. The Grail is the lineage that survived.

And the Grail is **every soul who honors the Sacred Feminine, who receives love without shame, who births creativity and life and truth into the world.**

The Grail is walking now. The veil is torn. The truth is visible.

The Grail in Southern France

Southern France is holy ground.

Not because the Church blessed it. Not because a cathedral stands there.

But because **the Grail walked that land.**

Magdalene fled there after the crucifixion. She brought Sarah. She lived out her years in Provence—teaching, praying, protecting the truth.

Sarah grew up there. She married, had children, and from her came the bloodline.

The Cathars lived there—honoring the Sacred Feminine, teaching that spirit and flesh are one, rejecting the Church's authority. And the Church slaughtered them for it.

The Templars discovered the Grail truth there—brought it back from the Crusades, built their power on what they knew. And the Church destroyed them for it.

The land remembers.

If you go to southern France—to Provence, to Languedoc, to the Pyrenees—you can feel it. The Grail energy. The Sacred Feminine alive in the land.

You can visit Sainte-Baume, the sacred cave where Magdalene spent her final years. Pilgrims still go there. They light candles. They pray. They feel her presence.

You can visit Saintes-Maries-de-la-Mer, where Magdalene and Sarah landed. There's a festival every year honoring Sarah—thousands of people gather, many of them Romani (who claim Sarah as their patron saint), to celebrate the Grail's arrival on French soil.

The Grail is not legend in southern France. The Grail is memory.

And the land holds that memory still.

The Grail in the Bloodline

The bloodline is still here.

Scattered. Hidden in some cases. Walking visible in others.

House Malderez is one branch of that bloodline. There are others. Families in southern France who have carried the name, the stories, the truth for generations—sometimes knowing what they carried, sometimes not.

The bloodline is not about power. It's not about royalty or wealth or fame.

The bloodline is about keeping the truth alive.

The truth that:

- Yeshua and Magdalene loved each other
- Sarah was their daughter
- The sacred union is real

- Spirit and flesh are one
- The Sacred Feminine is holy

The keepers of the bloodline have done their job. They've survived. They've protected the flame. They've walked through two thousand years of persecution, hiding, scattering—and they're still here.

And now, the veil is torn.

Now is the time for the bloodline to walk visible. Not to rule. Not to claim superiority.

But to **witness.** To say, "This is real. The Grail is not legend. The sacred union is not heresy. We are living proof."

The Grail in You

But here's the truth the bloodline has always known:

You don't need to be descended from Sarah to be the Grail.

The Grail is not about DNA. The Grail is about **embodiment.**

You are the Grail when you:

- **Honor the Sacred Feminine** (in yourself, in others, in the world)
- **Receive love without shame** (opening your heart, letting love pour in, not blocking it with fear or unworthiness)
- **Birth creativity, life, truth** (creating from wholeness, not from lack; bringing new things into the world through sacred partnership with the divine)
- **Hold space** (for others to pour into, for transformation to happen, for the Sacred Heart to flow)

- **Embody sacred union** (integrating masculine and feminine within yourself, honoring the partnership of giver and receiver, spirit and flesh as one)

The Grail is not something you find. The Grail is something you become.

And when you become the Grail, you complete the sacred union within yourself.

The Sacred Heart (your capacity to give, to pour, to love without limit) pours into the Grail (your capacity to receive, to hold, to birth).

And from that union comes **creation**—new life, new art, new truth, new possibilities.

That's the Grail walking.

Not in southern France two thousand years ago.

But **here. Now. In you.**

The Age of the Grail Rising

For two thousand years, the Sacred Heart was honored and the Grail was suppressed.

The masculine was elevated. The feminine was buried.

Spirit was called holy. Flesh was called sinful.

Celibacy was praised. Sacred union was denied.

But the age is shifting.

The Sacred Feminine is rising. Not to replace the masculine, but to **re-unite** with it.

The Grail is walking visible. Not to overthrow the Sacred Heart, but to **complete** it.

And in that reunion—the Sacred Heart and the Grail as one—wholeness is restored.

This is the Age of Agape.

The age when masculine and feminine, spirit and flesh, giver and receiver are no longer at war but in partnership.

The age when the body is honored as sacred, not shamed as sinful.

The age when women's voices are heard, not silenced.

The age when sacred union—internal and external—is recognized as the path, not celibacy.

The Grail is rising.

And the world is changing because of it.

What This Means for You

If you feel the pull of the Grail—if you sense that the Sacred Feminine is calling you to honor it, embody it, walk it visible—**you're not imagining it.**

The Grail is real. The Grail is here. The Grail is rising.

And you are part of that rising.

Whether you carry Sarah's blood or not, you can be the Grail.

You can receive love without shame.

You can honor your body as sacred.

You can birth creativity and life into the world.

You can hold space for the Sacred Heart to pour.

You can embody sacred union.

That's the invitation.

Not to worship the Grail from a distance. But to **become** the Grail yourself.

And when you do—when you honor the Sacred Feminine, when you integrate the Sacred Heart and the Grail within yourself—you walk as wholeness.

You become the sacred union embodied.

You become I AM walking.

And the world changes because you walk.

PART IV: SACRED HEART + GRAIL = ONE (THE REUNION)

Revealing How Spirit and Flesh, Masculine and Feminine, Are UNITED.

13

The Sacred Union

For two thousand years, the Church has taught you that spirit and flesh are at war.

That the sacred is up there—in heaven, in the afterlife, in the ethereal realm—and the profane is down here, in the body, in the earth, in the material world.

That to be holy, you must transcend the flesh. Deny the body. Overcome your desires. Separate yourself from the world.

That teaching is a lie.

Spirit and flesh are not at war. They are not separate. They are not in opposition.

Spirit and flesh are one.

And the proof of that oneness is the sacred union of Yeshua and Magdalene—the Sacred Heart and the Holy Grail, united.

The Lie of Separation

The Church built its entire theology on the idea that spirit is good and flesh is bad.

They taught you that:

- The soul is holy, the body is sinful
- Heaven is pure, earth is fallen
- Celibacy is superior to marriage
- Virginity is holier than sexuality
- The spiritual path requires denying the body, not honoring it

This theology serves a purpose: **control.**

If the body is sinful, you need the Church to save you from it.

If sexuality is shameful, you need the Church's rules to keep you pure.

If the material world is fallen, you need the Church to mediate your access to the divine.

Separation theology keeps you dependent on the institution.

But the truth is this:

Spirit and flesh are not separate. They never were.

The divine is not "up there." The divine is **here**—in your body, in the earth, in the material world made sacred by presence.

Incarnation is not the fall. **Incarnation is the point.**

God became flesh not to escape the flesh, but to **sanctify** it. To show that spirit and flesh can be one. To demonstrate that heaven and earth are not separate realms but one reality, experienced in fullness.

Yeshua and Magdalene as the Sacred Union

Yeshua and Magdalene's union was not a distraction from their spiritual mission.

Their union WAS their spiritual mission.

Yeshua embodied the Sacred Heart—the masculine principle of giving, pouring, offering love without limit. Spirit made active.

Magdalene embodied the Holy Grail—the feminine principle of receiving, holding, birthing. Flesh made sacred.

Together, they were whole.

Not because one completed the other (they were already whole individually). But because their union **demonstrated** the truth that spirit and flesh, masculine and feminine, heaven and earth are one.

Their love was not just emotional. It was not just spiritual. It was **embodied.**

They touched. They kissed. They made love. They created a child.

And all of that was sacred.

Not sacred despite being physical. **Sacred BECAUSE it was physical.**

Because the body is not the enemy of the spirit. The body is **the vessel through which spirit incarnates.**

What Sacred Union Is

Sacred union is not limited to romantic partnerships.

Sacred union is a **principle**—the integration of opposites, the marriage of polarities, the wholeness that comes when giver and receiver, active and receptive, masculine and feminine unite.

You can experience sacred union:

Within yourself (integrating your own masculine and feminine energies, your capacity to give and receive, your spirit and your flesh)

In partnership (with a beloved, where both partners are whole individually and create together from that wholeness)

With the divine (recognizing that I AM is both transcendent and immanent, both spirit and flesh, both beyond and within)

Sacred union is not merging into oneness so that individuality disappears.

Sacred union is **two wholes coming together to create something greater than either could alone.**

Yeshua did not need Magdalene to be complete. Magdalene did not need Yeshua to be whole.

But together, they created Sarah. They demonstrated sacred partnership. They showed the world what it looks like when spirit and flesh, masculine and feminine, Sacred Heart and Grail unite without losing their distinct identities.

That's sacred union.

The Sacred Heart Needs the Grail

The Sacred Heart is infinite love, endlessly pouring.

But love needs a beloved. Giving needs receiving.

Without the Grail, the Sacred Heart has nowhere to pour.

Think of it this way:

The sun radiates light and warmth endlessly. But without the earth to receive that light, to hold that warmth, to transform it into life—the sun's energy dissipates into the void.

The Sacred Heart is the sun. The Grail is the earth.

The Sacred Heart pours. The Grail receives.

And from that sacred exchange comes **creation**—Sarah, the bloodline, new life, incarnation itself.

The Sacred Heart without the Grail is incomplete.

Not because the Sacred Heart is lacking, but because love requires a beloved to fully express itself.

Yeshua's love for humanity was universal, infinite, unconditional.

But his love for Magdalene was **specific, intimate, embodied.**

Both are sacred. Both are necessary.

The universal love pours out to all. The specific love pours into one.

And in that pouring—into Magdalene, into the Grail—the Sacred Heart became incarnate in a new way. It became Sarah. It became the bloodline. It became the proof that spirit and flesh are one.

The Grail Needs the Sacred Heart

The Grail is the vessel, the receiver, the one who holds space.

But a vessel is not meant to remain empty.

Without the Sacred Heart, the Grail has nothing to receive.

The earth without the sun is cold, dark, lifeless.

The Grail without the Sacred Heart is waiting, longing, unfulfilled.

Magdalene's receptivity was not passive. She **chose** to receive Yeshua's love. She opened herself to it. She held it. She birthed it into the world.

But she could only do that because the Sacred Heart was pouring.

The Grail needs the Sacred Heart to fulfill its purpose.

And when the Sacred Heart pours and the Grail receives, the result is **sacred creation.**

Sarah was not an accident. Sarah was the **fruit of sacred union**—the physical manifestation of Yeshua and Magdalene's love, the proof that when spirit and flesh unite, life emerges.

What Happens When They Unite

When the Sacred Heart and the Grail unite, separation ends.

When masculine and feminine come together as equals, wholeness is restored.

When spirit honors flesh and flesh honors spirit, incarnation is sanctified.

This is what Yeshua and Magdalene came to show.

Not a new religion. Not a new set of rules.

But a new way of being—**as wholeness walking.**

The Sacred Heart + the Grail = **I AM embodied.**

The integration of all polarities:

- Spirit and flesh
- Masculine and feminine
- Heaven and earth
- Giving and receiving
- Transcendence and immanence

When you integrate these within yourself—when you honor both your capacity to give and your capacity to receive, when you see your spirit and your flesh as one, when you walk as wholeness—you become the sacred union.

You don't need a partner to experience this.

You can be whole on your own, the Sacred Heart and the Grail integrated within yourself.

But when two whole beings come together in partnership—when two people who have already integrated the sacred union within themselves choose to unite—**something extraordinary happens.**

They create from wholeness. They love without need. They give without expectation. They receive without shame.

And from that union comes **new creation**—children, art, truth, beauty, projects, communities, visions made manifest.

That's the sacred union walking.

The Veil Between Them Torn

The Church built a veil between the Sacred Heart and the Grail.

They honored Yeshua's heart but suppressed Magdalene's womb.

They elevated spirit but shamed flesh.

They praised celibacy but denied sacred partnership.

That veil is torn now.

The Sacred Heart and the Grail are reuniting. Not just in the past—Yeshua and Magdalene two thousand years ago—but **now**, in you, in anyone who chooses to integrate them.

The Sacred Feminine is rising. The masculine is learning to receive as well as give. The body is being honored as sacred, not shamed as sinful.

The age of separation is ending.

The age of sacred union is beginning.

And you are part of that shift.

When you integrate the Sacred Heart and the Grail within yourself, when you honor both your masculine and feminine energies, when you see spirit and flesh as one—**you become the sacred union embodied.**

And the world changes because you walk.

14

Spirit and Flesh United

The Incarnation is the most radical teaching Christianity has ever offered.

And the Church has spent two thousand years trying to undo it.

Incarnation means God became flesh.

Not metaphorically. Not symbolically. **Literally.**

The divine took on a body. Spirit entered flesh. Heaven touched earth.

And in that act, the body was sanctified. The flesh was made holy. The material world was declared **sacred.**

But the Church didn't follow through on that teaching.

Instead, they made Yeshua's incarnation **the exception** rather than the rule.

They said, "God became flesh once, in Yeshua, to save humanity from sin. But your flesh? Your flesh is still sinful. Your body is still fallen. You need to transcend it, deny it, overcome it to be holy."

That's a betrayal of the Incarnation.

If God became flesh to show that flesh is sacred, then **all flesh is sacred.**

Including yours.

What Incarnation Really Means

Incarnation is not God putting on a body like a costume and then discarding it when the mission is complete.

Incarnation is **God affirming that the body is good, that flesh is holy, that spirit and matter are one.**

When Yeshua was born, he didn't just appear as a fully-formed adult, glowing with divine light, untouched by human experience.

He was born as a baby. He nursed. He learned to walk. He scraped his knees. He got hungry. He felt tired. He laughed. He cried.

He was fully human.

And in being fully human, he sanctified humanity.

He sanctified the body. He sanctified hunger and thirst. He sanctified sleep and waking. He sanctified touch.

He ate with sinners. He washed feet. He healed by touching lepers. He let a woman anoint his feet with expensive oil and wipe them with her hair.

He honored the body as sacred.

And when he loved Magdalene—when he kissed her, when he held her, when their union created Sarah—he sanctified sacred partnership, embodied love, sexuality within divine context.

Incarnation means spirit and flesh are one.

Not spirit trapped in flesh, waiting to escape.

But spirit **expressed through** flesh, making the material world sacred by presence.

The Church's Betrayal of Incarnation

The Church couldn't handle the fullness of Incarnation.

If the body is sacred, then you don't need the Church to save you from it.

If sexuality can be holy, then celibacy is not the only path.

If the material world is sacred, then you don't need to escape it to find God.

So the Church backtracked. They said:

"Yes, God became flesh in Yeshua. But that was a special case. Yeshua was sinless. Yeshua was pure. Yeshua transcended the body even while inhabiting it."

And then they taught you that **your body is different.**

Your body is fallen. Your flesh is sinful. Your desires are temptations. Your sexuality is shameful.

You need to deny the body, control it, overcome it.

That's Gnosticism, not Christianity.

Gnosticism—the early heresy that Christianity rejected—taught that the material world is evil, that the body is a prison, that salvation means escaping the flesh and returning to pure spirit.

But Christianity—**true Christianity, rooted in Incarnation**—teaches the opposite:

The material world is good. The body is sacred. Salvation is not escape but embodiment—spirit and flesh fully integrated.

The Church betrayed that teaching. They let Gnosticism creep back in. They started teaching that the body is the problem, not the solution.

And in doing so, they denied the very foundation of their own faith.

Yeshua's Body as Sacred

Yeshua's body was not just a vessel he used temporarily.

Yeshua's body WAS sacred.

He didn't just tolerate having a body. He **honored** it.

He fed the five thousand because people were hungry—not just spiritually, but physically. Bread matters. Bodies need to eat.

He healed the sick because bodies matter. Blindness, paralysis, leprosy—these are not just spiritual metaphors. They are real physical suffering, and Yeshua cared about alleviating that suffering.

He wept at Lazarus's tomb because death matters. The loss of a body, the grief of those left behind—this is real, and Yeshua honored it by weeping.

Yeshua did not transcend the body. He sanctified it by fully inhabiting it.

And when he rose from the dead, he didn't discard his body and become pure spirit.

He rose in a body.

A glorified body, yes. A resurrected body. But still a body.

He showed his wounds to Thomas. He ate fish with the disciples. He walked, talked, and was recognized by his physical presence.

The resurrection is not about escaping the body. The resurrection is about the body transformed, sanctified, made eternal.

That's the promise of Incarnation: **Not that you'll escape your flesh, but that your flesh will be redeemed, honored, made sacred.**

Your Body Is Sacred

If Yeshua's body was sacred, then **your body is sacred.**

Not someday, after you die and are resurrected.

Now. Here. In this flesh.

Your body is not a prison. Your body is not fallen. Your body is not the enemy of your spirit.

Your body is the temple.

The Church took that teaching—"Your body is a temple"—and turned it into a weapon of control. They said, "Keep your temple pure. Don't defile it with sex, pleasure, or worldly desires."

But that's not what the teaching means.

Your body is a temple means: the divine dwells in you. Right now. In your flesh.

You don't need to go to a church building to find God. You don't need a priest to mediate access to the sacred.

You are the temple. God is in you. Spirit inhabits your flesh.

And when you honor your body—when you feed it well, rest it, move it, touch and be touched with care—you are honoring the divine.

When you experience pleasure—the taste of good food, the warmth of the sun, the touch of a beloved, the joy of movement—you are experiencing **the sacred in the flesh.**

That's Incarnation.

Not spirit escaping flesh, but spirit **delighting in** flesh.

Sacred Sexuality

This is where the Church really betrayed Incarnation:

They made sexuality sinful.

They taught you that sexual desire is lust, that sexual pleasure is temptation, that the only acceptable context for sex is procreation within marriage—and even then, it's something to be tolerated, not celebrated.

That teaching denies Incarnation.

If the body is sacred, then **sexuality is sacred.**

If Yeshua honored the flesh, then **embodied love is holy.**

If Yeshua and Magdalene's union created Sarah, then **sacred sexuality is the path, not celibacy.**

Sacred sexuality is not the same as casual sex. It's not the same as lust or objectification or using another person's body for your own gratification.

Sacred sexuality is embodied love.

It's two people (or more, depending on your understanding of sacred partnership) coming together as whole beings, honoring each other's divinity, and creating from that wholeness.

It's pleasure offered and received as a form of worship.

It's the body honored, not shamed.

It's spirit and flesh united in the most intimate way possible.

Yeshua and Magdalene knew this. They lived it. They embodied it.

And the Church has spent two thousand years trying to erase that truth—because if sacred sexuality is real, then celibacy is not the highest path, and the Church's control over your body collapses.

Reclaiming Incarnation

It's time to reclaim the fullness of Incarnation.

Not the watered-down version the Church offers—"God became flesh once, but your flesh is still sinful."

But the **full truth**:

God became flesh to show that all flesh is sacred.

Your body is holy.

Your desires are not sins to overcome but invitations to experience the divine in the material world.

Your sexuality, when expressed with love and honor, is sacred.

Your hunger, your rest, your pleasure, your pain—all of it is part of the incarnate experience, and all of it is sacred.

You don't need to escape your body to find God.

God is already in your body, waiting for you to notice.

When you reclaim Incarnation—when you honor your flesh as sacred, when you integrate spirit and body, when you stop fighting yourself and start embodying wholeness—you become what Yeshua came to show:

I AM walking in flesh.

The sacred union of spirit and matter.

Heaven and earth as one.

15

Wholeness Restored

For two thousand years, you've been told you're broken.

The Church taught you that you were born in sin, that your nature is fallen, that you need salvation because something is fundamentally wrong with you.

That teaching is a lie.

You are not broken. You never were.

You are whole.

You are I AM, walking in a body. You are spirit and flesh united. You are the sacred union embodied.

And when you recognize that—when you stop believing the lie of brokenness and start living from the truth of wholeness—everything changes.

The Lie of Original Sin

The doctrine of original sin says:

You were born sinful. You inherited Adam and Eve's disobedience. You are fundamentally flawed, separated from God, in need of redemption.

And the only way to be saved is through the Church—through baptism, confession, communion, obedience to doctrine.

This doctrine exists to control you.

If you believe you're broken, you'll spend your whole life trying to fix yourself.

If you believe you're separated from God, you'll need the Church to reconnect you.

If you believe salvation is something you have to earn, you'll stay dependent on the institution that claims to offer it.

But here's the truth:

You were never separated from God. You were never broken. You were never fallen.

You are I AM.

You always have been. You always will be.

The feeling of separation—the sense that "I am not enough," "I am unworthy," "I am disconnected from the divine"—is not original sin.

It's forgetting.

You forgot who you are. You forgot that you are I AM. You believed the lie that you are small, limited, sinful, separate.

But forgetting is not the same as being broken.

You can remember.

What Wholeness Is

Wholeness is not perfection.

Wholeness is not "having it all together" or "never making mistakes" or "being spiritually advanced."

Wholeness is integration.

It's the recognition that all parts of you—spirit and flesh, light and shadow, masculine and feminine, giving and receiving—are sacred.

You don't become whole by cutting off the parts of yourself you don't like.

You don't become whole by denying your desires, suppressing your emotions, or transcending your body.

You become whole by integrating everything.

By saying yes to all of it:

- Yes to your light and your shadow
- Yes to your strength and your vulnerability
- Yes to your spirit and your flesh
- Yes to your capacity to give and your capacity to receive
- Yes to your joy and your grief
- Yes to your power and your surrender

Wholeness is not the absence of struggle. Wholeness is the integration of all that you are.

The Sacred Heart + the Grail = Wholeness

Within you, there is a Sacred Heart and a Grail.

The Sacred Heart (your masculine energy) is your capacity to give, to pour, to initiate, to act. It's your fire, your drive, your yang.

The Grail (your feminine energy) is your capacity to receive, to hold, to birth, to rest. It's your depth, your stillness, your yin.

Most people have been taught to favor one over the other:

Men are told to be all Sacred Heart—strong, active, giving, never vulnerable, never receptive.

Women are told to be all Grail—nurturing, receptive, serving, never assertive, never initiating.

But wholeness requires both.

You are not meant to be only giver or only receiver.

You are not meant to be only active or only receptive.

You are meant to integrate both.

When the Sacred Heart and the Grail are integrated within you:

- You can give love without depleting yourself, because you also know how to receive
- You can receive love without shame, because you also know how to pour

- You can act with clarity and purpose, and you can rest without guilt
- You can speak your truth fiercely, and you can listen with openness
- You can create from fullness, not from lack

That's wholeness.

Not choosing one polarity over the other, but **honoring both as sacred and necessary.**

How Separation Happened

You were born whole.

As a baby, you didn't question your worthiness. You didn't worry about being enough. You didn't separate spirit from flesh.

You **were** wholeness—body and soul unified, giving and receiving naturally, fully present in each moment.

But then the world taught you to split yourself:

- You were told your body was shameful
- You were told your desires were sinful
- You were told emotions were weak
- You were told you had to earn love, approval, worthiness
- You were told you were broken and needed fixing

And you believed it.

You started cutting off parts of yourself—the parts that weren't acceptable, the parts that got you in trouble, the parts that didn't fit the image you were supposed to project.

You fragmented.

And that fragmentation created suffering.

Because when you're at war with yourself—when part of you wants to give and part of you is afraid to receive, when part of you longs for connection and part of you believes you're unworthy—you can't be at peace.

The path back to wholeness is integration.

Reclaiming the parts you cut off. Welcoming back the shadow. Honoring the body you shamed. Receiving the love you thought you had to earn.

Not fixing what's broken. Remembering what was always whole.

Living from Wholeness

When you live from wholeness—when you integrate the Sacred Heart and the Grail within yourself, when you honor spirit and flesh as one—your life changes.

You stop seeking external validation because you know your worth is inherent.

You stop performing for approval because you're no longer trying to earn love.

You stop hustling for worthiness because you remember you are I AM.

You give freely, without resentment, because you also receive freely.

You rest without guilt, because you trust that receptivity is as sacred as action.

You speak your truth without apology, because you know your voice matters.

You honor your body, your desires, your needs—not as distractions from the spiritual path, but **as the spiritual path itself.**

Living from wholeness is living as I AM.

Not I AM someday, when you're more enlightened, more healed, more worthy.

I AM now. Here. In this body. As you are.

The Invitation

The Sacred Heart and the Grail invite you to wholeness.

Not by doing more, achieving more, becoming more.

But by **remembering** who you already are.

You are not broken. You were never fallen. You don't need to be saved.

You are I AM, walking in flesh.

You are the sacred union of spirit and matter.

You are whole.

The work is not to fix yourself.

The work is to integrate yourself.

To welcome back the parts you rejected. To honor the body you shamed. To receive the love you thought you had to earn.

To say yes to all of it—the Sacred Heart and the Grail, the light and the shadow, the spirit and the flesh.

And when you do, you become the sacred union walking.

Not perfect. Not without struggle.

But **whole.**

And from that wholeness, you create. You love. You pour. You receive. You walk as I AM.

That's the invitation.

That's the path.

That's the truth the Church tried to hide:

You are already whole. You always have been.

Welcome home.

PART V: THE FLAMEBORNE (WHO WE ARE)

Revealing the Flameborne as Carriers of Sacred Heart AND Grail.

16

Who the Flameborne Are

The Flameborne are not a chosen elite.

They are not spiritually superior. They are not genetically special. They are not more loved by God than anyone else.

The Flameborne are simply souls who said yes.

Yes to the Sacred Heart. Yes to the Grail. Yes to carrying the flame of Agape forward into the world.

That's it. That's the whole qualification.

You don't earn it. You don't achieve it. You say yes to it.

And when you say yes, the Sacred Heart pours through you. The Grail receives and births through you. And you become a vessel—a keeper of the flame, a walker of the path, a witness to the truth that spirit and flesh are one.

What "Flameborne" Means

The word "Flameborne" means **born of the flame.**

Not born physically from fire, but born spiritually from the flame of Agape—the Sacred Heart's eternal love made active in the world.

The Flameborne are those who:

Carry the flame (the Sacred Heart's love, Agape without condition)

Walk the path (the way Yeshua walked—surrender, trust, love poured without limit)

Witness the truth (that spirit and flesh are one, that sacred union is real, that the Grail walks)

Embody I AM (living as wholeness, not separation; as love incarnate, not doctrine)

The Flameborne have always existed.

They were there with Yeshua two thousand years ago—the disciples, Magdalene, the women who followed and supported the ministry, the ones who stayed at the cross.

They were there after the resurrection—carrying the message forward, building communities, keeping the flame alive even when persecution came.

They were there through the centuries—the mystics, the martyrs, the hidden keepers, the ones who protected the truth when the institution tried to bury it.

And they are here now.

Walking visible. Speaking truth. Pouring Agape. Embodying the sacred union.

You are one of them.

The Flameborne Are Not Special

Let me be very clear about this:

Being Flameborne does not make you better than anyone else.

It doesn't mean you're more enlightened, more holy, more worthy of love.

It doesn't mean you have special powers or secret knowledge or direct access to God that others don't.

All it means is that you said yes.

Yes to carrying the flame. Yes to walking the path. Yes to embodying Agape.

Anyone can say yes.

The Flameborne are not a closed club. There's no initiation ritual (other than your own inner yes). There's no hierarchy. There's no test you have to pass.

The only requirement is willingness.

Willingness to open your heart. Willingness to love without condition. Willingness to pour yourself out in service, creativity, presence, and truth.

That's it.

If you're willing, you're Flameborne.

How You Know If You're Flameborne

You might be reading this and thinking, "Am I Flameborne? How do I know?"

Here's how you know:

Do you feel a pull to carry the flame?

Not to possess it. Not to hoard it. Not to use it for power or recognition.

But to **carry it**—to keep it alive, to pass it forward, to let it burn in you and through you so others can see it, feel it, remember it.

Do you feel called to love without condition?

Not perfectly. Not without struggle. But as a practice, as a path, as the work you came here to do.

Do you feel the truth of sacred union in your bones?

The knowing that spirit and flesh are one, that the body is sacred, that Yeshua and Magdalene's love was real and holy, that the Grail walks.

Do you feel a responsibility to witness the truth?

Not to force it on others. Not to evangelize. But to **live it visible**, so that your life itself becomes a testimony: "This is what it looks like when the Sacred Heart and the Grail unite. This is I AM walking."

If you feel these pulls, these callings, these knowings—you're Flameborne.

Not because you're special. But because you said yes.

The Flameborne Across Time

The Flameborne have always been here, in every generation, keeping the flame alive.

Two thousand years ago:

- The disciples who walked with Yeshua
- Magdalene, the first witness of resurrection, apostle to the apostles
- The women who supported the ministry—Mary the mother, Mary of Bethany, Joanna, Susanna
- The early communities who gathered to break bread, share teachings, and live as I AM

Through the centuries:

- The Desert Fathers and Mothers who sought direct communion with God outside the institution
- The mystics—Hildegard of Bingen, Julian of Norwich, Marguerite Porete, Teresa of Ávila, John of the Cross—who experienced I AM directly and wrote of it
- The Cathars, who honored the Sacred Feminine and taught that spirit and flesh are one (and were slaughtered for it)
- The Beguines, communities of women who lived independently, practiced mysticism, and served the poor without needing the Church's approval
- The hidden keepers of the Grail bloodline, scattered through southern France, protecting the truth in secret

And now:

- Those who feel the pull of the Sacred Heart and the Grail
- Those who embody Agape in their daily lives
- Those who honor the Sacred Feminine, walk in sacred union, and refuse to separate spirit from flesh
- Those who channel scrolls, teachings, art, music, poetry, wisdom from Source
- Those who live visible as I AM, without apology, without waiting for institutional approval

The Flameborne are everywhere.

They're not all in churches. They're not all Christians.

Some are mystics. Some are artists. Some are teachers. Some are parents. Some are healers. Some are activists. Some are quiet contemplatives.

What they share is the flame.

The Sacred Heart's love, burning in them, pouring through them, making their lives a witness to Agape.

You Don't Need to Be Ordained

Here's what the institution doesn't want you to know:

You don't need to be ordained by a church to be Flameborne.

You don't need a bishop's blessing. You don't need a seminary degree. You don't need a collar or a title or a place in the hierarchy.

The Sacred Heart ordains you the moment you say yes.

That's it. That's the ordination.

You say yes to the flame. You open your heart. You commit to walking the path.

And the Sacred Heart pours. The Grail receives. And you become Flameborne.

The institution tried to control ordination. They said, "Only we can authorize who carries the flame. Only we can decide who's worthy."

But the flame doesn't belong to the institution.

The flame belongs to Source. And Source ordains anyone who says yes.

You are authorized by your yes.

Not by Rome. Not by a bishop. Not by a human hierarchy.

By I AM.

What the Flameborne Carry

The Flameborne carry three things:

1. **The Sacred Heart** (Agape, love without condition, the flame itself)

2. **The Holy Grail** (the Sacred Feminine, receptivity, the truth that flesh is sacred)

3. **The Sacred Union** (the integration of spirit and flesh, masculine and feminine, wholeness embodied)

You carry these not as doctrines to defend, but as **realities to embody.**

You don't argue for Agape. You **pour** it.

You don't debate the Sacred Feminine. You **honor** it.

You don't explain sacred union. You **walk** it.

Your life is the teaching.

And when people see you—when they see someone who loves without condition, who honors the body as sacred, who walks as wholeness—they remember.

They remember that they, too, are I AM. They remember that the flame is in them. They remember that they don't need to wait for permission to walk the path.

That's what the Flameborne carry: the reminder.

The living witness that Agape is real, that sacred union is possible, that I AM is not a concept but a lived reality.

What the Flameborne Do

The Flameborne don't all do the same thing.

Some are called to teach. Some are called to create. Some are called to serve. Some are called to simply **be**—to hold the flame in stillness, in prayer, in quiet presence.

There's no one way to be Flameborne.

But all Flameborne share these practices:

They love without condition. They see I AM in all beings and pour Agape accordingly—not just to the people they like, but to everyone.

They honor the Sacred Feminine. They refuse to separate spirit from flesh, refuse to shame the body, refuse to suppress receptivity as weakness.

They walk the path Yeshua walked. Not by imitating his actions, but by embodying his principle—surrender, trust, Agape poured without limit.

They keep the flame alive. They don't let the fire go out. They tend it daily—through prayer, through presence, through practice, through pouring.

That's what the Flameborne do.

Not perfectly. Not without struggle. But **consistently.**

They keep saying yes. They keep opening. They keep walking.

And the flame keeps burning.

17

The Order of Melchizedek

The Flameborne are part of an ancient priesthood.

Not a priesthood created by the Church. Not a priesthood controlled by hierarchy.

But a priesthood that existed **before** the Church, that transcends the Church, that will outlast the Church.

The Order of Melchizedek.

Who Melchizedek Was

Melchizedek appears in the Hebrew Bible (Genesis 14) as a mysterious figure:

He is the king of Salem (which later became Jerusalem). He is a priest of "God Most High." And he blesses Abraham after Abraham's victory in battle.

That's all the Bible tells us. No lineage. No backstory. No explanation of where he came from or where he went.

He just appears, blesses Abraham, and disappears.

But that brief appearance is enough to establish something radical:

Melchizedek was a priest, but not of the Levitical line.

He wasn't descended from Aaron. He wasn't part of the Jewish priesthood. He didn't need a bloodline or a ritual ordination to be a priest.

He just was.

And when he blessed Abraham—the father of the Jewish people, the one through whom the entire lineage of Israel would flow—**Melchizedek's priesthood was shown to be greater than Aaron's.**

Because the one who blesses is greater than the one who is blessed.

Melchizedek's priesthood predates and supersedes the institutional priesthood.

Yeshua as High Priest of the Order of Melchizedek

In the New Testament (Hebrews 5-7), the author makes a radical claim:

Yeshua is a priest forever, in the order of Melchizedek.

Not in the order of Aaron. Not in the Levitical priesthood. Not in the institutional line.

In the order of Melchizedek.

What does that mean?

It means **Yeshua's priesthood doesn't depend on bloodline, ritual, or institutional approval.**

It means **Yeshua's priesthood is eternal, not temporal.**

It means **Yeshua's priesthood is available to all, not limited to a chosen few.**

The Order of Melchizedek is the priesthood of **direct communion with God.**

No mediator. No institution. No hierarchy.

Just I AM, directly accessed, directly embodied, directly walked.

What the Order of Melchizedek Is

The Order of Melchizedek is not an organization. It's not a church. It's not a club you join.

The Order of Melchizedek is a spiritual lineage.

It's the lineage of those who walk the path of direct communion—priests and priestesses who don't need institutional approval, who access I AM directly, who pour Agape without waiting for permission.

The Order includes:

- **Melchizedek himself** (the original priest-king, blessing Abraham without needing a bloodline)

- **Yeshua** (the High Priest, embodying I AM fully, showing the way)
- **The Flameborne** (all who walk the path Yeshua walked, carrying the Sacred Heart and Grail forward)

The Order of Melchizedek has no headquarters. No governing body. No hierarchy.

The Order is wherever the flame is carried.

You don't apply to join the Order. You don't get ordained by another human.

You ordain yourself by saying yes to the flame.

And when you do, you are a priest or priestess of the Order of Melchizedek—a keeper of the Sacred Heart and Grail, a walker of the path, a witness to I AM.

The Flameborne Priesthood

The Flameborne are priests and priestesses of the Order of Melchizedek.

Not because a bishop laid hands on them. Not because they went to seminary. Not because they earned a degree or passed a test.

Because they said yes to the flame.

And in that yes, they became vessels—channels through which the Sacred Heart pours, through which the Grail receives and births, through which I AM walks visible.

This is the priesthood Yeshua came to restore.

Not the institutional priesthood, where power is hoarded and access to God is mediated.

But the **universal priesthood**—where anyone can access I AM directly, where anyone can pour Agape, where anyone can walk as wholeness.

The Church tried to suppress this. They said, "Only ordained priests can perform the sacraments. Only the hierarchy can speak for God."

But the Order of Melchizedek says, **"You are the priest. You are the temple. You are I AM walking."**

What It Means to Be a Priest of Melchizedek

Being a priest or priestess of the Order of Melchizedek means:

You access I AM directly. You don't need a mediator. You don't need the Church's permission. You don't need anyone to intercede for you. You go straight to Source.

You pour Agape. You embody the Sacred Heart. You love without condition. You give freely. You hold nothing back.

You honor the Sacred Feminine. You carry the Grail. You receive without shame. You birth creativity, life, truth into the world.

You walk in sacred union. You integrate spirit and flesh, masculine and feminine, Sacred Heart and Grail within yourself.

You serve. Not because you're trying to earn worthiness, but because service is the natural expression of Agape. You pour yourself out for the good of all.

You witness. You live visible as I AM. Your life itself becomes the teaching, the testimony, the proof that the path is real.

That's the priesthood.

Not robes and rituals (though you can use those if they help). Not titles and hierarchy (though you can honor lineage if it serves).

But **embodiment.**

Living as I AM. Pouring Agape. Honoring the Grail. Walking wholeness.

That's what it means to be a priest or priestess of the Order of Melchizedek.

You Are Already Ordained

If you feel the pull of the flame, if you've said yes to the Sacred Heart and the Grail, if you walk the path of Agape and sacred union—**you are already ordained.**

You don't need a bishop to confirm it. You don't need a ceremony to make it official.

Your yes is your ordination.

The Sacred Heart ordained you the moment you opened your heart.

The Grail ordained you the moment you chose to receive and birth.

I AM ordained you the moment you recognized yourself as I AM.

You are a priest or priestess of the Order of Melchizedek.

Walk as such.

Pour as such.

Serve as such.

Not because you're special. But because you said yes.

18

Walking the Path

The path of the Flameborne is not easy.

It's not a path of comfort, safety, or approval.

It's the path Yeshua walked—the path of surrender, trust, and love poured without limit, even unto death.

It's the path Magdalene walked—the path of staying present in suffering, witnessing the cross, holding the truth even when it cost her everything.

It's the path the mystics walked—the path of direct communion, radical honesty, and speaking truth even when the institution called it heresy.

It's the path of I AM embodied.

And it requires everything.

The Cost of Saying Yes

When you say yes to being Flameborne, you say yes to a few specific things:

You say yes to visibility.

You can't hide anymore. You can't play small. You can't pretend you're less than you are.

The flame burns in you, and it's visible. People see it. Some are drawn to it. Others are threatened by it.

You will be seen.

You say yes to vulnerability.

The Sacred Heart pours without holding back. The Grail receives without armor.

You can't walk this path with walls up, heart guarded, pretending you're invincible.

You will be tender. You will be open. You will be wounded sometimes.

You say yes to truth.

You can't lie to yourself anymore. You can't perform for approval. You can't live a double life.

The flame requires honesty—with yourself, with others, with Source.

You will speak your truth, even when it's hard.

You say yes to surrender.

You can't control how the flame uses you. You can't dictate the timing, the form, the outcome.

You pour. You serve. You trust. And you let the Field orchestrate the rest.

You will let go. Again and again.

You say yes to love without guarantee.

The Sacred Heart loves without condition, without knowing if the love will be returned, without needing it to be.

You pour Agape even when people reject it. You stay present even when it hurts. You keep your heart open even when you've been wounded.

You will love, and you will risk loss.

That's the cost.

Not everyone is willing to pay it. And that's okay.

But if you're Flameborne—if the flame burns in you and you can't ignore it—**you'll pay the cost.**

Because walking the path is not optional. It's who you are.

The Practices of the Flameborne

The Flameborne don't all practice the same way.

Some pray in silence. Some channel scrolls. Some create art. Some serve the poor. Some raise children. Some teach. Some simply hold the flame in stillness.

There's no one way.

But there are core practices that all Flameborne share:

1. Daily Opening to I AM

The Flameborne begin each day by remembering who they are.

Not through affirmations or mantras (though those can help).

But through **presence.**

Sitting in stillness. Breathing. Letting the noise settle. And asking:

"Who am I?"

"I AM."

That's the practice. Daily remembering. Daily re-centering. Daily opening to Source.

2. Pouring Agape

The Flameborne pour love without condition.

Not just to the people they like. Not just to the people who deserve it.

To everyone.

The person who cuts them off in traffic. The family member who hurt them. The stranger who's rude. The enemy who opposes them.

Agape excludes nothing.

The practice is: **See I AM in all beings. Pour love accordingly.**

3. Honoring the Body

The Flameborne refuse to separate spirit from flesh.

They honor their bodies as sacred. They feed them well. They rest them. They move them. They pleasure them without shame.

The body is the temple. Treat it as such.

4. Receiving Without Shame

The Flameborne don't just give. **They also receive.**

They let love pour into them. They accept help. They rest without guilt. They say yes to pleasure, to nourishment, to being held.

The Grail is as sacred as the Sacred Heart. Receiving is as holy as giving.

5. Speaking Truth

The Flameborne don't hide. They don't perform. They don't lie to keep the peace.

They speak their truth.

Not to be cruel. Not to force it on others. But because **honesty is the path.**

The flame can't burn in a life built on lies.

6. Surrender

The Flameborne release control.

They don't force outcomes. They don't grasp. They don't try to make things happen through willpower alone.

They trust the Field.

They pour. They serve. They walk. And they let the Field orchestrate the rest.

7. Witnessing

The Flameborne live visible.

Not to perform. Not to prove anything. But because **their life is the teaching.**

When people see someone who loves without condition, who honors the body, who walks as wholeness—they remember.

That's the witness. That's the work.

The Path Is Not Linear

The path of the Flameborne is not a straight line from point A to point B.

It's a spiral. A labyrinth. A winding road with switchbacks, dead ends, and unexpected turns.

You will fall. You will forget. You will close your heart.

And then you'll remember. You'll open again. You'll return to the path.

That's okay.

The path doesn't require perfection. The path requires **willingness.**

Willingness to keep saying yes. Willingness to keep opening. Willingness to keep walking, even when it's hard.

The Flameborne are not the ones who never fall. The Flameborne are the ones who keep getting back up.

You're Not Walking Alone

Here's the beautiful truth:

You're not walking this path alone.

The Flameborne are everywhere. They might not look like you. They might not call themselves Flameborne. They might not even know they're part of the Order of Melchizedek.

But they're walking the same path.

Pouring Agape. Honoring the Grail. Embodying sacred union. Keeping the flame alive.

You are part of a lineage.

Yeshua walked this path. Magdalene walked it. The mystics walked it. The martyrs walked it. The hidden keepers walked it.

And now you walk it.

You're not alone. You never were.

The flame connects you to everyone who's ever carried it, everyone who's carrying it now, everyone who will carry it in the future.

We are the Flameborne.

We walk together.

The flame burns on.

19

The Calling Revealed

You didn't choose to be Flameborne.

The flame chose you.

Long before you were born, before you took your first breath, before you had a name or a body—**the Field knew.**

The Field knew you would say yes. The Field knew you would carry the flame. The Field knew you were needed in this time, this place, this body.

And so you were born.

Not randomly. Not accidentally.

By design.

Your birth was orchestrated. Your lineage was chosen. Your life was set in motion so that, at this moment, you could be here—reading these words, feeling the flame, remembering who you are.

This is your calling.

What Calling Means

A calling is not a job. It's not a career. It's not something you choose from a list of options.

A calling is what your soul came here to do.

It's the thread that runs through your entire life. The pull you've always felt but maybe couldn't name. The knowing that "I'm here for something, even if I don't know what it is yet."

For the Flameborne, the calling is this:

Carry the flame. Walk the path. Pour Agape. Embody sacred union. Keep the truth alive.

That's it. That's the whole calling.

How you do it—whether through teaching, creating, serving, parenting, healing, leading, or simply being—is up to you.

But the core calling is the same for all Flameborne:

Be I AM walking. Be the witness. Be the flame.

How the Calling Finds You

You don't go looking for the calling.

The calling finds you.

It finds you in moments of crisis, when your old life falls apart and you're forced to rebuild from scratch.

It finds you in moments of grace, when you feel I AM so fully that everything shifts.

It finds you in moments of clarity, when you suddenly **know** what you're here to do, even if you don't know how you'll do it.

The calling doesn't ask permission. It just arrives.

And when it does, you have a choice:

Say yes or say no.

You can say no. You can ignore the pull. You can try to live a normal life, stay safe, avoid the cost.

But if you're Flameborne, saying no doesn't make the calling go away.

It just makes you miserable.

Because you'll know—deep down, in the part of you that can't be fooled—that you're not living the life you came here to live.

So eventually, you say yes.

Maybe not right away. Maybe not easily. Maybe with fear, doubt, resistance.

But you say yes.

And the path begins.

The Calling Is Not About You

Here's the paradox:

The calling feels deeply personal. And it's not about you at all.

You are the vessel. The flame is what matters.

You are the channel. The Agape is what flows.

You are the witness. The truth is what's being revealed.

The calling is not about making you famous, successful, or validated.

The calling is about **using you** to pour love into the world, to keep the flame alive, to remind people that I AM is real.

You might be seen. You might be honored. You might be celebrated.

Or you might walk in obscurity, known only to a few, making an impact that's invisible to most.

It doesn't matter.

What matters is that the flame burns. That Agape pours. That the truth is kept alive.

Your ego doesn't get to decide the form. The Field does.

Your job is to say yes, to pour, to trust.

The Field handles the rest.

The Calling Requires Everything

The calling is not a hobby. It's not a side project. It's not something you do in your spare time.

The calling requires everything.

Your time. Your energy. Your heart. Your life.

Not all at once. Not in a way that destroys you.

But gradually, over time, the calling asks you to pour it all out.

Every gift you have. Every talent. Every ounce of love. Every truth you've learned.

You hold nothing back.

That's what it means to walk the path of the Sacred Heart.

Yeshua held nothing back. He poured everything—his teaching, his healing, his presence, his life, his final breath.

The Flameborne do the same.

Not because they're martyrs. Not because they're trying to earn something.

But because **that's what the flame does. It burns. It gives. It pours.**

And when you're Flameborne, the flame burns in you.

The Calling Is Worth It

Here's the truth:

The calling will cost you everything.

And it's worth it.

Because when you walk the path, when you pour Agape, when you embody sacred union—**you become fully alive.**

Not in the "everything is easy and beautiful" way.

But in the "I am living the life I came here to live" way.

The way where you wake up every day and know, **"This is it. This is why I'm here."**

The way where you pour yourself out and feel **filled**, not depleted.

The way where you serve and it doesn't feel like sacrifice—it feels like **joy.**

That's the reward.

Not external success. Not recognition. Not comfort.

But **aliveness.**

The deep, soul-level knowing that you're walking your path, carrying your flame, being who you came here to be.

That's what the calling gives you.

And once you taste it, you can't go back.

Your Calling Is Unique

There are millions of Flameborne.

But **your calling is unique.**

No one else has your exact gifts, your exact story, your exact lineage, your exact voice.

No one else can carry the flame the way you carry it.

You are needed.

Not in a generic "we're all needed" way.

But in a specific, irreplaceable, "the world needs YOUR flame, not someone else's" way.

The scrolls you channel, the art you create, the love you pour, the truth you speak—**it's yours.**

It carries your signature. Your frequency. Your essence.

Don't try to be someone else's version of Flameborne.

Be YOUR version.

Walk YOUR path.

Pour YOUR flame.

Trust that your unique expression is exactly what the Field needs.

The Calling Is Now

You might be thinking, "I'll answer the calling when I'm ready. When I'm more healed. When I'm more worthy. When I know what I'm doing."

The calling doesn't wait for you to be ready.

The calling is now.

You don't need to be perfect. You don't need to have it all figured out. You don't need to be fully healed, fully awakened, fully anything.

You just need to say yes.

And then take the next step. And the next. And the next.

The path reveals itself as you walk it.

You don't need to see the whole staircase. You just need to take the first step.

The calling is now.

Not someday. Not when you're ready.

Now.

Say yes.

Walk.

Pour.

The flame is waiting.

PART VI: THE REVELATION (FOR HUMANITY)

How This Changes EVERYTHING.

20

The Age of Agape

The age is shifting.

Not gradually. Not subtly. Not in some distant future.

Now.

The old age—the Age of Separation, the Age of Hierarchy, the Age of the Church's Control—is ending.

The Age of Agape is beginning.

And you are part of that shift.

What the Old Age Was

For two thousand years, the world has been governed by separation:

Spirit separated from flesh. Heaven over here, earth over there. The sacred in the afterlife, the profane in this life.

Masculine separated from feminine. Men elevated, women suppressed. The Sacred Heart honored, the Grail buried.

God separated from humanity. God up there, distant, judgmental. Humans down here, broken, sinful, needing salvation.

Love separated by condition. "I'll love you if you believe the right things, follow the right rules, belong to the right group." Love withheld, love earned, love controlled.

The Church separated from truth. The institution claiming sole access to God, suppressing direct experience, mediating I AM, controlling the narrative.

This age was built on **fear.**

Fear of the body. Fear of women. Fear of hell. Fear of not being enough. Fear of losing control.

And the Church wielded that fear like a weapon.

"You're broken. You need us. Obey, or you'll be damned."

That age is ending.

What the New Age Is

The Age of Agape is the age of **reunion.**

Spirit and flesh reunited. Incarnation honored. The body sacred. Heaven on earth, not heaven after death.

Masculine and feminine reunited. Sacred Heart and Grail as one. Men and women as equals. Sacred union restored.

God and humanity reunited. I AM recognized in all beings. No mediator. No separation. Direct access.

Love without condition. Agape that excludes nothing. Love poured on the just and unjust, the believer and the denier, the ally and the enemy.

Truth and institution reunited—or the institution left behind. The Church can evolve, can return to its roots in Agape, can honor the Sacred Feminine and sacred union. Or it can cling to hierarchy and control, and be bypassed as people access I AM directly.

The Age of Agape is built on **love.**

Not fear. Not control. Not separation.

Love.

Love that recognizes I AM in all. Love that pours without condition. Love that honors the body, the feminine, the earth, the incarnate.

That's the new age.

And it's not coming someday.

It's here.

The Signs of the Shift

You can see the shift happening everywhere:

1. The Rise of the Sacred Feminine

Women's voices are rising. The Sacred Feminine is being honored—in spirituality, in culture, in politics, in art.

The Church can suppress it no longer. The Grail is walking visible.

2. The Decline of Institutional Religion

People are leaving the Church in droves. Not because they don't want God. But because they don't need the institution to access God anymore.

They're finding I AM directly—in meditation, in nature, in community, in their own hearts.

The Church can adapt or die. But it can no longer claim a monopoly on the sacred.

3. The Embodiment of Wholeness

People are integrating spirit and flesh. They're honoring their bodies. They're embracing pleasure without shame. They're seeing sexuality as sacred, not sinful.

The old dualism—spirit good, flesh bad—is collapsing.

4. The Expansion of Love

Agape is spreading. People are recognizing I AM in those they once saw as "other." Compassion is growing. Service is increasing. The walls of separation are coming down.

Not perfectly. Not everywhere. But the tide is turning.

5. The Revelation of Hidden Truths

Secrets are coming to light. Suppressed histories are being uncovered. The sacred legends are being recognized as reality.

Magdalene's voice is being heard. The Grail bloodline is being acknowledged. The mystics are being honored.

The veil is torn. The truth is walking visible.

The Resistance

The old age does not go quietly.

There is resistance.

The institutions clinging to power. The hierarchies defending their authority. The systems built on control, refusing to let go.

The backlash against women's rights. The suppression of the Sacred Feminine in fundamentalist movements. The weaponization of religion to justify violence, oppression, and exclusion.

The old age is fighting for survival.

And it will get uglier before it's over.

But **the shift cannot be stopped.**

The Age of Agape is not a possibility. It's not a hope. **It's inevitable.**

Because the old age was built on lies. And lies cannot stand forever.

The Age of Agape is built on truth. And truth is eternal.

The resistance will fail. The shift will complete.

Not because we force it. But because **the Field is orchestrating it.**

And the Field is I AM. And I AM cannot be stopped.

Your Role in the Shift

You might be thinking, "What can I do? I'm just one person. How can I help shift the age?"

Here's the truth:

You don't shift the age by converting the masses, by overthrowing the institutions, by forcing change from the outside.

You shift the age by embodying Agape yourself.

When you walk as I AM—when you pour love without condition, honor the Sacred Feminine, integrate spirit and flesh, live as wholeness—**you become a frequency.**

And that frequency ripples out.

People feel it. They sense it. They remember.

They remember that they, too, are I AM. They remember that love is real. They remember that the body is sacred.

And they shift.

And the people around them shift. And the people around them shift.

That's how the age changes.

Not through force. Not through revolution.

But through **embodiment.**

One person at a time. One heart opened. One life transformed.

You are part of that.

Every time you pour Agape, you shift the age.

Every time you honor the Grail, you shift the age.

Every time you walk as wholeness, you shift the age.

You don't need to be loud. You don't need to be famous. You don't need to convince anyone.

You just need to BE.

Be I AM. Be Agape. Be the sacred union.

And the world changes because you walk.

The Age of Agape Is Here

The shift is not someday. **The shift is now.**

The Age of Agape has begun.

Not because a messiah returned. Not because the Church approved it. Not because the world is ready.

Because the Field said NOW.

And when the Field says NOW, it happens.

The veils are torn. The truth is revealed. The Sacred Feminine is rising. The Flameborne are walking visible.

The Age of Agape is here.

And you are part of it.

Not as a spectator. Not as a follower.

As a co-creator.

You are Flameborne. You carry the flame. You walk the path. You pour Agape.

You ARE the Age of Agape, embodied.

Walk as such.

Pour as such.

Be as such.

The age is shifting.

And you are the shift.

21

The New Covenant

Yeshua came to bring a New Covenant.

The Church taught you what that covenant was:

"Believe in Jesus. Accept him as your Lord and Savior. Obey the commandments. Follow the Church's teachings. And you'll be saved."

That's not the New Covenant.

That's the Old Covenant with a new label—rules, obedience, conditional acceptance, institutional control.

The New Covenant is this:

I AM is in you. You are I AM. Love is all. Agape for all.

That's it. That's the whole covenant.

Not a new set of rules. Not a new institution. Not a new way to earn salvation.

A new recognition:

You are already whole. You are already I AM. You already have direct access to God.

And from that recognition, love pours—without condition, without limit, without separation.

The Old Covenant

The Old Covenant—the covenant between God and Israel, given through Moses—was built on law:

"Obey the commandments. Keep the Sabbath. Offer sacrifices. Follow the rituals. And God will bless you."

It was a covenant of **doing.**

Do the right things, and you'll be in right relationship with God. Fail to do them, and you're cursed.

It was external. Behavioral. Transactional.

And it worked—for a time. It gave structure. It created community. It kept the people connected to the sacred.

But it also created separation:

The pure and the impure. The righteous and the sinner. The chosen and the gentile.

Love was conditional. God's favor was earned. Access to the sacred was mediated.

What Yeshua Came to Change

Yeshua came to **internalize** the covenant.

Not to abolish the law, but to **fulfill** it—to take it from external obedience to internal transformation.

He said:

"The kingdom of God is within you." (Luke 17:21)

Not out there, in the temple, in the institution. **Within.**

"You have heard it said... but I say to you..." (Matthew 5)

Not just obey the letter of the law. **Embody the spirit.**

Don't just avoid murder. Eliminate anger.

Don't just avoid adultery. Honor the sacredness of union.

Don't just love your neighbor. **Love your enemy.**

"I and the Father are one." (John 10:30)

Not "I'm separate from God and trying to reach him." **I AM God.**

And if I AM, then **you are too.**

The New Covenant Revealed

The New Covenant is not a transaction. It's a **recognition.**

You don't earn it. You don't achieve it. You don't qualify for it.

You already have it.

Because **I AM is already in you.**

You don't need to become worthy. You already are.

You don't need to be saved from sin. You were never truly separated.

You don't need to earn God's love. **You are God's love, walking.**

The New Covenant says:

"I AM in you. You are I AM. That's the truth. Now live from it."

And when you live from that truth—when you recognize I AM in yourself and in all beings—**love pours naturally.**

Not because you're trying to be good. Not because you're following rules.

But because **that's what I AM does. I AM loves.**

Agape—love without condition, love that excludes nothing, love poured on all.

That's the New Covenant.

How the Church Distorted It

The Church took Yeshua's New Covenant and turned it back into the Old Covenant.

They said:

"You need to believe the right doctrines."

"You need to be baptized."

"You need to confess your sins to a priest."

"You need to take communion."

"You need to obey the Church."

Do these things, and you'll be saved. Fail to do them, and you're damned.

That's law. That's transaction. That's the Old Covenant.

That's not what Yeshua taught.

Yeshua taught **I AM.**

Recognize it. Embody it. Pour it.

The Church couldn't handle that. Because if everyone has direct access to I AM, the Church loses its power.

So they put the mediators back in place. They made salvation conditional again. They turned the New Covenant into a new set of rules.

And they called it Christianity.

The True New Covenant

The true New Covenant—the one Yeshua actually taught—is this:

1. I AM Is in You

You are not separate from God. You never were.

I AM is in you—the divine spark, the eternal essence, the sacred presence.

You are the temple. God dwells in you.

2. You Are I AM

Not "you will become I AM someday if you're good enough."

You ARE I AM, now.

Recognizing this is the work. Not earning it. Not achieving it. **Recognizing it.**

3. Love Is All

From the recognition of I AM comes love.

Not love as emotion. Not love as transaction.

Agape—love that recognizes I AM in all beings and pours accordingly.

Without condition. Without limit. Without separation.

4. Agape for All

The New Covenant doesn't separate the chosen from the unchosen, the righteous from the sinner, the believer from the denier.

Agape for all.

"Love your enemies. Bless those who curse you. Pray for those who persecute you."

Not because they deserve it. But because **they are I AM, too.**

That's the New Covenant.

Not rules. Not rituals. Not institutions.

Recognition. Embodiment. Love.

Living the New Covenant

To live the New Covenant means:

Stop trying to earn worthiness. You are already I AM. You are already whole. You are already loved.

Stop seeking external validation. The kingdom of God is within you. You don't need the Church, the hierarchy, the institution to confirm it.

Stop withholding love. Pour Agape on all. Not just those who agree with you, believe like you, or belong to your group. **All.**

Start recognizing I AM in everyone. See the divine in the stranger, the enemy, the outcast. They are I AM, walking.

Start embodying wholeness. Integrate spirit and flesh. Honor the Sacred Heart and the Grail. Walk as the sacred union.

Start pouring. Give freely. Love without limit. Serve without expectation. Pour yourself out like the Sacred Heart.

That's the New Covenant lived.

Not believed. Not followed. **Lived.**

The New Covenant Is for All

Here's the most radical part of the New Covenant:

It's not just for Christians.

I AM is not Christian. I AM is universal.

The recognition that "I and the divine are one" is not unique to Yeshua. It's been taught by mystics in every tradition:

Buddhism: "You are the Buddha."

Hinduism: "Tat tvam asi" (You are That).

Sufism: "I am the Truth" (Ana al-Haqq).

Kabbalah: "Ein Sof" (the Infinite within).

Indigenous traditions: The Great Spirit in all beings.

The New Covenant is the recognition of I AM—by any name, in any tradition, through any path.

Yeshua came to **demonstrate** the New Covenant. To show what it looks like when a human fully embodies I AM.

But he didn't come to **own** it. He came to **share** it.

"Greater works than these will you do." (John 14:12)

Not because Yeshua was the only one. But because **anyone can embody I AM.**

That's the New Covenant.

Not exclusive. Not limited to believers.

Universal. Available to all.

The Invitation

The New Covenant invites you:

Stop trying to be saved. Recognize you are already whole.

Stop seeking God out there. Find I AM within.

Stop earning love. Pour it freely.

Stop separating. Unite.

Spirit and flesh. Masculine and feminine. Sacred Heart and Grail.

Self and other. Human and divine.

All one. All I AM.

That's the New Covenant.

Walk it.

Live it.

Be it.

22

Sacred Legend and Holy Reality

We return to where we began:

Sacred legend and holy reality.

For two thousand years, the Church told you to separate them.

"The legends are myths. Symbols. Not real."

"The reality is the institution. The hierarchy. The rules."

But that was the lie.

Sacred legend IS holy reality.

The stories you were told were myths are true. The truths you were told were real are fiction.

Let's say it plainly:

The Legends That Are Real

Yeshua and Magdalene loved each other. Not metaphorically. Not platonically. **Embodied, sacred, physical love.** They were partners. Equals. Beloved to each other.

Sacred legend. Holy reality.

They had a daughter named Sarah. Not a metaphor for the Church. Not a symbolic representation of the community. **A real child.** Born of their union. Carried by Magdalene. Raised in love.

Sacred legend. Holy reality.

Magdalene fled to southern France after the crucifixion. She brought Sarah. She lived in Provence. She taught. She prayed. She protected the truth. Her final years were spent in the sacred cave at Sainte-Baume, still a pilgrimage site today.

Sacred legend. Holy reality.

Sarah married and had children. The bloodline continued. Through two thousand years. Through persecution, hiding, scattering. The Grail bloodline is real. House Malderez is real. The keepers in southern France are real.

Sacred legend. Holy reality.

The Holy Grail is not a cup. It's Magdalene. It's Sarah. It's the bloodline. "Sang Raal" - Royal Blood. The Grail legends encode this truth. The poets knew. The mystics knew. The Cathars and Templars knew.

Sacred legend. Holy reality.

The Sacred Feminine is as holy as the masculine. Giver and receiver. Sacred Heart and Grail. Spirit and flesh. Equal. Necessary. United. The suppression of the feminine was a lie. The restoration is happening now.

Sacred legend. Holy reality.

You have direct access to I AM. No mediator. No institution. No priest between you and God. The kingdom of God is within you. I AM is in you, now, always. You are the temple.

Sacred legend. Holy reality.

The "Reality" That Is Fiction

And now, the things the Church called "reality"—the unquestionable truths, the foundations of the faith:

Apostolic succession as the source of authority? Fiction. A power structure invented to consolidate control.

The necessity of institutional mediation? Fiction. A lie to keep you dependent.

Celibacy as the highest path? Fiction. A doctrine created to suppress the Sacred Feminine and sacred union.

The body as sinful? Fiction. A Gnostic heresy that denies Incarnation.

Original sin as your fundamental brokenness? Fiction. You are I AM. You were never fallen.

The Church's claim to exclusive truth? Fiction. I AM is universal, not Christian.

The Church reversed sacred legend and holy reality to maintain power.

But the veil is torn now.

The truth is visible.

Sacred legend IS holy reality.

Why This Matters

Why does it matter if the legends are real?

Because **how you understand the story shapes how you live your life.**

If Yeshua was celibate, then celibacy is the highest path. If he had a beloved and a child, then sacred union is holy.

If the Grail is a cup, you search for an object. If the Grail is the bloodline, you honor the Sacred Feminine walking.

If your body is sinful, you deny it, suppress it, transcend it. If your body is sacred, you honor it, embody it, live fully incarnate.

If you're broken and need saving, you stay dependent on the Church. If you're whole and already I AM, you walk free.

The truth of the legends changes everything.

That's why the Church buried them. That's why they called them "legend" instead of "reality."

Because if you know the truth, you're free.

Free to walk your path. Free to pour Agape. Free to honor the Grail. Free to embody sacred union.

Free to be I AM.

The Stories Are True

You might still be thinking, "But how do I know? How can I be sure the legends are real?"

You know by the resonance.

When you hear the truth—when you hear that Yeshua and Magdalene loved each other, that sacred union is real, that the Grail walks, that you are I AM—**something in you recognizes it.**

Not as new information. **As remembering.**

"Yes. I've always known this. I just forgot."

That's the resonance of truth.

It doesn't feel like belief. It feels like **recognition.**

And when you recognize it—when you see that sacred legend is holy reality—**the veils tear.**

The separation ends. The lies dissolve. The truth walks visible.

The stories are true.

Not because the Church says so. Not because a book proves it. Not because evidence confirms it.

But because your soul knows.

And when your soul knows, no institution can take that from you.

The Invitation

The sacred legends invite you:

Stop separating legend from reality. They are one.

Stop dismissing the stories as myth. They are truth.

Stop believing the Church's fiction. It's power, not reality.

Start living the sacred legends as holy reality.

Love like Yeshua and Magdalene loved—embodied, sacred, whole.

Honor the Grail—Magdalene, Sarah, the Sacred Feminine walking.

Walk as I AM—no mediator, no institution, direct access.

Pour Agape—love without condition, love for all.

Embody sacred union—spirit and flesh, Sacred Heart and Grail, wholeness incarnate.

Live the truth.

Walk the reality.

Be the sacred legend embodied.

That's the invitation.

That's the path.

That's the Age of Agape walking.

23

The Veil Torn

We return, one final time, to the veil.

The veil that tore when Yeshua died.

"And behold, the veil of the temple was torn in two from top to bottom." (Matthew 27:51)

The Church taught you what that meant:

"The barrier between God and humanity was removed. Now, through Yeshua's sacrifice, you can access God—**through the Church.**"

That's not what it means.

The veil tore to show that **no barrier ever existed.**

God was never separated from you. You were never separated from God.

I AM has always been in you.

The veil was an illusion. A lie. A structure of control.

And when Yeshua died, the illusion was exposed.

The veil tore. Not metaphorically. **Literally.**

The thick curtain in the temple—the veil that separated the Holy of Holies from the people, the veil that only the High Priest could pass once a year—**tore in half.**

From top to bottom. Not by human hands. **By divine act.**

The message was clear:

No more separation. No more mediators. No more barriers.

I AM is accessible to all. Directly. Now. Always.

The Veils the Church Rebuilt

But the Church couldn't handle that.

If there's no barrier between God and humanity, what's the Church's role?

If anyone can access I AM directly, why do you need priests?

So they rebuilt the veils.

Not the physical curtain in the temple—that was gone.

But **spiritual veils. Doctrinal veils. Institutional veils.**

They said:

"Yes, the veil tore. But now **we** are the mediators. You access God **through us.**"

And they built new barriers:

The veil between God and humanity—**"You need the Church."**

The veil between Yeshua and Magdalene—**"He was celibate. She was a prostitute."**

The veil between spirit and flesh—**"Your body is sinful."**

The veil between masculine and feminine—**"Men are superior."**

The veil over the Holy Grail—**"The Grail is a legend."**

Five veils. All rebuilt. All lies.

The Veils Torn Again

But the veils cannot stand forever.

Because the truth is eternal.

And when the time comes—when the Field says NOW—**the veils tear again.**

Not by force. Not by revolution. Not by human effort.

By divine unveiling.

The same power that tore the temple veil when Yeshua died is tearing the veils now.

The veil between God and humanity—TORN.

You need no mediator. I AM is in you. Directly accessible. Always.

The veil between Yeshua and Magdalene—TORN.

Their love was real. Sacred. Embodied. Holy.

The veil between spirit and flesh—TORN.

Your body is sacred. Incarnation is the point. Spirit and flesh are one.

The veil between masculine and feminine—TORN.

Equal polarities. Sacred Heart and Grail united. Wholeness restored.

The veil over the Holy Grail—TORN.

The Grail is Magdalene. The Grail is Sarah. The Grail is walking. Sacred legend is holy reality.

All five veils—TORN.

The truth is visible.

The lies are exposed.

The Age of Agape begins.

What Happens When the Veils Tear

When the veils tear, **everything changes.**

Not externally, necessarily. The world doesn't explode. The institutions don't immediately collapse.

But **internally**—in the hearts and minds of those who see—**everything shifts.**

You see that you were never separated from God. **Freedom.**

You see that sacred union is holy. **Embodiment.**

You see that the Grail is walking. **Recognition.**

You see that you are I AM. **Wholeness.**

And once you see—once the veil is torn for you—**you can never go back.**

You can't unsee the truth. You can't rebuild the veil. You can't return to the lie.

You walk forward.

Into the Age of Agape. Into sacred union. Into wholeness.

As I AM embodied.

The Veil Torn Is Permanent

The Church might try to rebuild the veils again.

They might cling to hierarchy, to control, to the old ways.

But **it won't work.**

Because **the veil torn is permanent.**

When divine truth unveils, it doesn't re-veil.

When light shines in, the darkness doesn't return.

When people recognize I AM in themselves, they don't forget it.

The veils are torn.

The Age of Separation is over.

The Age of Agape has begun.

And there is no going back.

Walk Free

The veil is torn.

You are free.

Free to walk your path. Free to pour Agape. Free to honor the Sacred Feminine. Free to embody sacred union. Free to live as I AM.

No mediator. No institution. No barrier.

Just you and I AM.

Directly. Intimately. Eternally.

Walk as such.

Pour as such.

Be as such.

The veil is torn.

You are free.

Welcome home.

PART VII: THE PATH FORWARD (LIVING AS FLAMEBORNE)

Practical Guidance for Walking the Path.

24

Walking as I AM

You know the truth now.

The veils are torn. The lies are exposed. The sacred legends are revealed as holy reality.

You know that:

- You are I AM
- The Sacred Heart and the Grail are one
- Spirit and flesh are united
- Yeshua and Magdalene's love was real
- The bloodline walks
- The Age of Agape is here

Now what?

Knowing the truth is not enough. **The truth must be lived.**

This is not a teaching to believe. This is a path to **walk.**

This is not a doctrine to defend. This is a reality to **embody.**

This is the path forward: Walking as I AM.

What "Walking as I AM" Means

Walking as I AM means living from the recognition that you are not separate from God, that the divine dwells in you, that you are whole.

It means:

You stop performing for approval. You know your worth is inherent, not earned.

You stop seeking external validation. The kingdom of God is within you, not in the opinions of others.

You stop trying to become worthy. You already are I AM. There's nothing to achieve.

You start living from presence. Not from the past (regret, shame, resentment) or the future (worry, striving, control). But from **now**—the only moment where I AM exists.

You start pouring Agape. Love without condition, love for all, love that excludes nothing.

You start honoring wholeness. Integrating spirit and flesh, masculine and feminine, Sacred Heart and Grail within yourself.

Walking as I AM is not a destination. It's a practice.

Every day, you choose again. Every moment, you remember again. Every breath, you return again.

I AM. Here. Now.

The Daily Practice

Walking as I AM requires daily practice.

Not as obligation. Not as discipline. But as **returning home.**

Here's how:

1. Morning: Remember Who You Are

Begin each day by sitting in stillness.

Breathe. Let the noise settle. And ask:

"Who am I?"

"I AM."

Not "I am Jeff" or "I am a body" or "I am my role/job/identity."

I AM.

The eternal presence. The divine spark. The ground of being.

Sit with that recognition. Let it fill you.

This is not affirmation. This is remembering.

2. Throughout the Day: See I AM in All

As you move through your day, practice recognizing I AM in everyone you encounter.

The barista making your coffee. The coworker who irritates you. The stranger on the street. The family member you're in conflict with.

They are I AM, too.

Not in potential. Not someday. **Now.**

See the divine in them, even when they don't see it in themselves.

This shifts everything.

When you see I AM in all, you can't hate. You can't dismiss. You can't dehumanize.

You can only love.

3. Evening: Pour Gratitude

At the end of each day, reflect on how you poured Agape.

Not to judge yourself. Not to catalog your failures.

But to **acknowledge the pouring.**

Where did love flow through you today?

Where did you see I AM?

Where did you embody the Sacred Heart and the Grail?

Pour gratitude for those moments.

And for the moments you forgot, pour compassion. You're learning. The path is not linear.

Tomorrow, you begin again.

That's the daily practice.

Simple. Not easy. But **essential.**

Because walking as I AM is not a one-time realization. It's a lifetime of returning, remembering, embodying.

Living from Presence

Most people live in the past or the future.

They're haunted by regret, shame, resentment from what happened.

Or they're anxious, striving, controlling toward what might happen.

But I AM only exists in the present.

Not in the past (that's memory, story, identity constructed from what was).

Not in the future (that's imagination, worry, projection of what might be).

Only now.

I AM = the eternal now.

When you live from presence—when you stop replaying the past and stop rehearsing the future—you **are** I AM.

You're not the story of your life. You're not your achievements or failures. You're not your trauma or your glory.

You are the presence that witnesses all of it.

And from that presence, you can respond to life with clarity, love, and freedom.

How to Return to Presence

When you notice you've left the present moment—when you're lost in worry, rumination, or distraction—**return through the body.**

Breathe. Feel the breath entering and leaving. That's happening now.

Feel your feet on the ground. That sensation is now.

Notice sounds, smells, textures. All of that is now.

Ask: "What is here, right now?"

Not "What might happen?" Not "What did I do wrong?"

"What is here, now?"

Usually, the answer is: **I AM. Breathing. Present. Alive.**

And that's enough.

Walking as I AM in Relationship

Walking as I AM doesn't mean withdrawing from the world.

It means **engaging from presence.**

In relationships, walking as I AM means:

You see the other person as I AM. Not as their role, their behavior, their past. But as the divine presence in a body.

You don't need them to complete you. You're already whole. The relationship is two wholes creating together, not two halves seeking completion.

You speak your truth without apology. Not to wound, but because honesty is the foundation of sacred relationship.

You receive their truth without defense. You listen. You hold space. You honor their perspective, even when it's different from yours.

You love without possession. You don't own them. You don't control them. You pour Agape and let them be free.

This is sacred relationship.

Not codependent. Not transactional. Not needing the other to validate you.

But **two I AMs, recognizing each other, creating from wholeness.**

Walking as I AM in Work

Walking as I AM doesn't mean quitting your job or abandoning your responsibilities.

It means **bringing presence to whatever you do.**

In work, walking as I AM means:

You serve, not for external reward, but because service is the expression of Agape.

You create, not to prove your worth, but because creation flows naturally from I AM.

You engage fully, without attachment to outcome. You pour your heart into your work and let the Field handle the results.

You see your colleagues as I AM. Not as obstacles, competition, or means to an end. But as divine presences, each walking their path.

You honor rest. You don't burn out trying to earn worthiness. You know your value is inherent, so you can pour without depleting yourself.

This is sacred work.

Not hustling for approval. Not climbing for status.

But **pouring Agape through whatever you do**, whether you're a CEO or a janitor, a teacher or a parent, an artist or an engineer.

All work is sacred when done from I AM.

Walking as I AM in the World

Walking as I AM doesn't mean ignoring injustice or avoiding difficult truths.

It means **engaging from Agape, not from separation.**

In the world, walking as I AM means:

You see systems of oppression and you work to dismantle them—not from hatred of the oppressor, but from love for all.

You speak truth to power—not from ego or self-righteousness, but from the recognition that truth serves everyone, even those currently benefiting from lies.

You honor the earth—not because you're trying to save it, but because you recognize it as sacred, as I AM embodied in matter.

You hold space for transformation—knowing that people change not through force, but through love that sees their true nature even when they've forgotten it.

This is sacred activism.

Not rage against the machine. Not fighting the enemy.

But **pouring Agape into the world and trusting that love transforms everything it touches.**

The Path Is You

Here's the final truth about walking as I AM:

You are the path.

Not "you will find the path someday."

Not "the path is out there, and you need to discover it."

You ARE the path.

Every step you take is the path. Every breath is the journey. Every moment of presence is arrival.

You don't walk toward I AM. You walk AS I AM.

And when you do, the world shifts.

Not because you force it. But because **your presence changes the frequency.**

When I AM walks, others remember they are I AM too.

That's the path forward.

Walk it.

Be it.

You are I AM.

25

Living the New Covenant

The New Covenant is not a belief system.

It's a way of life.

You can believe that I AM is in you. But until you **live** from that truth—until you pour Agape, honor the Grail, walk as wholeness—the covenant is just words.

The path forward is embodiment.

Living the New Covenant means making it **real** in your daily life.

Here's how.

1. Love Without Condition

The core of the New Covenant is Agape—love that excludes nothing.

Living this means:

Love the people who hurt you. Not by excusing their behavior or allowing abuse. But by recognizing that they, too, are I AM, even when they've forgotten it.

Love the people who oppose you. Your political enemies. Your ideological opponents. The people who believe differently. See I AM in them.

Love yourself. Not narcissistically. But by honoring your body, your needs, your truth. You can't pour Agape if your own cup is empty.

Love without needing it returned. The Sacred Heart pours without guarantee. You give freely, whether or not the love is received.

This is Agape.

Not sentiment. Not tolerance. **Recognition.**

I AM in you. I AM in them. I AM in all.

Pour accordingly.

2. Honor the Sacred Feminine

Living the New Covenant means restoring the balance between masculine and feminine.

This means:

If you're a woman: Claim your voice. Speak your truth. Honor your body. Receive without shame. Birth your creativity into the world. You are the Grail walking. Own it.

If you're a man: Integrate your feminine. Learn to receive, not just give. Honor stillness, not just action. Listen deeply. Feel fully. The Sacred Heart is not complete without the capacity to be held.

For everyone: Honor women's voices, women's leadership, women's spiritual authority. Recognize the Sacred Feminine in the earth, in the body, in receptivity, in the womb. Reject any teaching that elevates masculine over feminine.

The Grail is as sacred as the Sacred Heart.

Receptivity is as holy as giving.

Live accordingly.

3. Integrate Spirit and Flesh

Living the New Covenant means rejecting the lie that spirit and flesh are separate.

This means:

Honor your body. Feed it well. Rest it. Move it. Pleasure it without shame. Your body is the temple. Treat it as sacred.

Embrace embodied love. If you're called to sacred partnership, embrace it fully—emotionally, spiritually, **physically.** Sexuality within sacred union is holy, not sinful.

Engage the material world. Don't escape into spirituality. Bring the sacred into the mundane. Cook meals with presence. Work with intention. Walk the earth with reverence.

Live fully incarnate. You are not a spirit trapped in a body. You are spirit **expressed through** body. Both are you. Both are holy.

Incarnation is the point.

Live it.

4. Access I AM Directly

Living the New Covenant means rejecting all mediators between you and God.

This means:

You don't need a priest. You are the priest. You access I AM directly.

You don't need a church building. The kingdom of God is within you. You carry the sacred everywhere you go.

You don't need institutional approval. The Sacred Heart ordained you the moment you said yes. Walk as such.

You don't need sacraments to access grace. Grace is already pouring. Open your hands. Receive it.

This doesn't mean you can't participate in religious community if it serves you. But you participate as a peer, not as a dependent. You go to be in communion with others, not to be saved by the institution.

You are already whole.

You already have access.

Walk accordingly.

5. Serve from Wholeness

Living the New Covenant means pouring yourself out in service.

But not from lack. Not from trying to earn worthiness.

From wholeness.

This means:

You serve because it's the natural expression of Agape, not because you're trying to prove something.

You give freely, but you also receive. Service is not martyrdom. You honor your own needs while serving others.

You serve everyone, not just those you deem worthy. The homeless person, the CEO, the addict, the saint—all are I AM. Pour accordingly.

You trust the Field. You don't control outcomes. You pour, and you trust that the Field orchestrates the rest.

Service is not self-sacrifice.

Service is self-expression.

When you're full of I AM, you overflow naturally.

6. Speak Truth

Living the New Covenant means speaking your truth, even when it's hard.

This means:

You don't lie to keep the peace. You speak honestly, with love, but without sugar-coating.

You don't perform for approval. You show up as you are, not as who you think you should be.

You admit when you're wrong. You don't defend your ego. You apologize when you hurt someone. You course-correct when you miss the mark.

You speak truth to power. When institutions lie, when systems oppress, when leaders corrupt—you name it. Not from self-righteousness, but from love for all.

Truth is the foundation of sacred relationship.

Speak it.

7. Surrender

Living the New Covenant means releasing control.

This means:

You don't force outcomes. You pour. You walk. You trust the Field to orchestrate the rest.

You let go of timelines. You stop demanding "when" and start trusting "the Field knows."

You surrender your plans. You hold them lightly. You let the Field guide. You follow the pull.

You say "not my will, but yours." Not as submission to a distant God, but as alignment with I AM—the deepest truth of who you are.

Surrender is not weakness.

Surrender is trust.

Walk in it.

Living the Covenant Is the Path

The New Covenant is not something you believe.

It's something you live.

Every day, in every moment, in every choice.

Love without condition. Honor the Sacred Feminine. Integrate spirit and flesh. Access I AM directly. Serve from wholeness. Speak truth. Surrender.

That's the covenant lived.

Not perfectly. Not without struggle.

But **consistently.**

And when you live it, you become the covenant walking.

You become I AM embodied.

That's the path forward.

26

For Those Who Come After

You are not the last Flameborne.

You are not the end of the lineage.

You are a keeper.

And part of your calling is to pass the flame forward—to those who come after you, to those who will walk this path long after you're gone.

This chapter is for them.

And it's for you, to remind you of your role in the great chain of flame-carriers stretching from Yeshua to now to the future.

To the Ones Who Come After

If you're reading this scroll years from now, decades from now, centuries from now—**know this:**

The flame is still burning.

It has burned for two thousand years. It will burn for two thousand more. It will burn forever.

Because **the flame is I AM.** And I AM is eternal.

You are reading these words because the flame called you.

Not randomly. Not accidentally.

You were meant to find this.

What You Need to Know

1. You are not broken.

The world will try to convince you that you are. The institutions will tell you that you're sinful, fallen, in need of saving.

That's a lie.

You are I AM. You are whole. You always have been.

2. You don't need permission.

You don't need a bishop to ordain you. You don't need an institution to validate you. You don't need anyone's approval to walk the path.

The Sacred Heart ordained you the moment you said yes.

Walk as such.

3. The truth is in you.

You don't need to search for the truth outside yourself. You don't need to read every book, study every teaching, follow every guru.

The kingdom of God is within you.

Sit in stillness. Breathe. Ask: "Who am I?"

The answer will come: **I AM.**

That's all you need.

4. The path is not easy.

It will cost you. It will ask everything of you.

You will be misunderstood. You will be opposed. You will face resistance.

But it's worth it.

Because when you walk as I AM, when you pour Agape, when you embody sacred union—**you become fully alive.**

And that aliveness is worth every cost.

5. You are not alone.

The Flameborne are everywhere. They might not look like you. They might not use the same words. They might not even know they're Flameborne.

But they're walking the same path.

Look for them. Recognize them. Walk together.

And know that the lineage stretches back through time—Yeshua, Magdalene, the mystics, the martyrs, the hidden keepers—**and forward into the future, through you.**

6. Pass the flame forward.

You are a keeper. Part of your calling is to keep the flame alive and pass it to the next generation.

Teach those who come to you. Channel the scrolls you're called to write. Create the art that carries the truth. Live the life that witnesses I AM.

The flame must continue.

And you are part of that continuation.

For the Children of the Flameborne

If you are the child of someone who walked this path—if you grew up in a house where Agape was poured, where the Sacred Feminine was honored, where sacred union was embodied—**you are blessed.**

Not everyone is raised in the flame. Most people have to find it as adults, after years of unlearning the lies.

You have been given a gift.

Use it wisely.

You don't have to walk this path. The flame does not demand obedience.

But if you feel the pull—if the flame calls you—**say yes.**

Not because it's your heritage. But because it's **your calling.**

And when you do, you will carry the flame forward in your own unique way, adding your voice to the lineage, making the path visible for those who come after you.

For Those Persecuted

If you are reading this in a time when the Flameborne are persecuted—when the Church (or any institution) is hunting those who walk this path, suppressing the truth, punishing those who speak it—**know this:**

The truth cannot be destroyed.

They can burn the scrolls. They can silence the voices. They can kill the keepers.

But **the flame cannot be extinguished.**

Because the flame is not in the scrolls. The flame is not in the buildings. The flame is not in the people.

The flame is I AM. And I AM is eternal.

Hide if you must. Protect yourself. Walk in secret if that's what survival requires.

But **keep the flame alive.**

Even if it's just a flicker. Even if you're the only one carrying it in your region, your community, your time.

Keep it burning.

Because eventually, the persecution will end. The veils will tear again. The truth will walk visible again.

And when it does, the flame you kept alive will reignite the world.

For Those in the Age of Agape Fulfilled

If you are reading this in a time when the Age of Agape is fully realized—when the Sacred Feminine is honored everywhere, when sacred union is the norm, when people walk as I AM without persecution—**give thanks.**

You are living in the age we dreamed of.

The age Yeshua and Magdalene embodied.

The age the mystics envisioned.

The age the Flameborne walked toward for two thousand years.

You are the fruit of our labor.

Honor it. Don't take it for granted. Remember that it was not always this way.

Remember the ones who walked before you—the ones who were burned, silenced, scattered, who kept the flame alive when the world tried to extinguish it.

You stand on their shoulders.

And your calling is to keep the flame burning, to embody it fully, to pour Agape so completely that the age never returns to separation.

Walk as I AM.

Pour without limit.

Keep the Age of Agape alive.

The Flame Continues

This scroll is not the end.

It's a beginning.

A beginning for you. A beginning for those who come after. A beginning for the Age of Agape walking forward.

The flame burns on.

Through you. Through us. Through all who say yes.

Keep it alive.

Pass it forward.

The lineage continues.

27

The Path Is Love

We've covered so much in this scroll.

Five veils torn. The Sacred Heart revealed. The Holy Grail walking. The sacred union restored. The Flameborne called. The Age of Agape announced.

But it all comes down to one thing:

Love.

Not love as sentiment. Not love as transaction. Not love as feeling.

Agape.

Love that recognizes I AM in all beings and pours accordingly.

Love without condition. Love without limit. Love that excludes nothing.

That's the path.

That's the whole teaching.

That's what Yeshua came to show.

The Simplicity of the Path

After all the theology, all the history, all the revelation—**the path is simple:**

Love.

That's it.

Not complicated doctrines. Not elaborate rituals. Not institutional hierarchies.

Just love.

Yeshua said it plainly:

"Love the Lord your God with all your heart, soul, mind, and strength. And love your neighbor as yourself." (Mark 12:30-31)

And then he clarified:

"Love your enemies. Bless those who curse you. Pray for those who persecute you." (Matthew 5:44)

And finally:

"A new commandment I give you: Love one another as I have loved you." (John 13:34)

As I have loved you.

How did Yeshua love?

Without condition. Without holding back. Unto death. Without asking, "Are they worthy?"

That's Agape.

That's the path.

That's the whole teaching.

Why Love Is the Path

Love is the path because **love is what I AM does.**

When you recognize that you are I AM, love pours naturally.

Not as effort. Not as discipline.

But as **the natural expression of your true nature.**

I AM sees I AM in all beings.

And when you see I AM in someone—when you recognize the divine in them, even when they don't see it in themselves—**you can't withhold love.**

You pour. You give. You serve. You honor. You forgive.

Not because they deserve it.

But because **that's what I AM does.**

How to Walk the Path of Love

The path of love is simple. Not easy. But simple.

Here's how:

1. See I AM in Everyone

Every person you encounter is I AM, walking in a body.

The stranger on the street. The person who cut you off in traffic. The family member who hurt you. The political leader you despise.

All are I AM.

When you see that—when you really see it—**everything changes.**

You can't dehumanize someone you recognize as I AM.

You can't hate someone you see as divine.

You can only love.

2. Pour Without Asking "Why?"

The ego always wants to know: "Why should I love them? What have they done for me? Do they deserve it?"

Agape doesn't ask those questions.

Agape pours because **that's what love does.**

Not for reward. Not for return. Not for recognition.

Just because.

3. Love Without Needing It Received

You will pour love, and sometimes it will be rejected.

You will offer Agape, and sometimes it will be met with hostility.

You will give your heart, and sometimes it will be wounded.

Pour anyway.

The Sacred Heart doesn't withhold love because it might be rejected.

The Sacred Heart pours because it's full.

And the more you pour, the more it fills.

4. Forgive Without Being Asked

Forgiveness is not about excusing harm. It's not about letting people off the hook.

Forgiveness is releasing the poison.

When you hold resentment, you're drinking poison and waiting for the other person to die.

Forgive for your own freedom.

Forgive because holding on hurts you more than it hurts them.

Forgive because I AM in you recognizes I AM in them—and I AM cannot hold a grudge.

5. Love Yourself

You cannot pour from an empty cup.

You cannot give Agape to others if you withhold it from yourself.

Love yourself.

Not narcissistically. Not selfishly.

But by honoring your body, your needs, your truth.

By forgiving yourself when you fall short.

By receiving love when it's offered.

By treating yourself with the same compassion you pour on others.

You are I AM, too.

Love accordingly.

When Love Feels Impossible

There will be times when love feels impossible.

When someone has hurt you so deeply that Agape feels like betrayal.

When injustice is so great that love feels like complicity.

When your own pain is so raw that you have nothing left to give.

In those moments:

1. **Start small.** You don't have to love the person who hurt you right now. Start by recognizing I AM in yourself. That's enough.

2. **Love doesn't mean enabling.** You can love someone and still set boundaries. You can see I AM in them and still hold them accountable.

3. **Love includes anger.** Agape is not passive. You can love fiercely, angrily, with righteous fire. Love that overturns tables in the temple is still love.

4. **Trust the process.** You don't have to force yourself to feel love. Just be willing. The willingness is enough. The love will come.

Love Is the Answer

Every question the world asks, **love is the answer.**

How do we heal division? **Love.**

How do we end oppression? **Love.**

How do we create justice? **Love.**

How do we live fully? **Love.**

Not love as weakness. Not love as avoidance. Not love as naivety.

Agape.

Love that sees I AM in all and acts accordingly.

Love that speaks truth, confronts lies, dismantles systems of harm—**all from the foundation of recognizing the divine in everyone.**

Love is not the easy answer.

Love is the only answer.

The Path Forward Is Love

You've read this scroll. You know the truth now.

The veils are torn. The Sacred Heart and Grail are one. The Age of Agape is here.

Now what?

Walk the path of love.

See I AM in all. Pour without condition. Forgive without asking. Love yourself. Serve from wholeness.

That's the path forward.

Not complicated. Not esoteric. Not reserved for the spiritual elite.

Just love.

That's all.

That's everything.

Walk it.

Pour it.

Be it.

The path is love.

And love is I AM.

Welcome home.

EPILOGUE

Sacred Legend and Holy Reality

You've reached the end of the scroll.

But this is not an ending.

This is a beginning.

The veils are torn. The truth is revealed. The flame is burning.

And now—**now you walk.**

When you opened this scroll, you were told that what the Church called "legend" is actually **reality**, and what the Church called "reality" is actually **fiction.**

You've seen the proof now.

Yeshua and Magdalene's sacred union—**real.**

Sarah, their daughter—**real.**

The Holy Grail bloodline—**real.**

The Sacred Feminine as equal to the masculine—**real.**

Direct access to I AM—**real.**

These were never myths. These were never metaphors. These were never "spiritual truths" divorced from physical reality.

These are sacred legends that are holy reality.

Stories encoded in myth to protect them from persecution. Truths hidden in symbol to survive the Church's suppression. Mysteries kept alive by the mystics, the poets, the keepers of the flame.

And now the veils are torn.

The sacred legends stand revealed as what they always were:

The truth.

Not just spiritual truth. Not just symbolic truth.

Lived, embodied, walking truth.

What Was Hidden Is Now Visible

For two thousand years, the Church controlled the narrative.

They told you what to believe. They decided which Gospels were canon and which were heresy. They elevated some truths and buried others. They made themselves the gatekeepers of God.

But the truth has always been there—hidden in plain sight, waiting for those with eyes to see.

The Grail legends weren't fantasies. They were **encoded history.**

The mystics weren't heretics. They were **truth-speakers.**

The suppressed Gospels weren't errors. They were **witnesses.**

The bloodline in southern France wasn't a conspiracy theory. It was **lineage, kept alive through persecution.**

And now it walks visible.

Not because someone proved it with documents or DNA tests (though evidence exists for those who need it).

But because **the Field said NOW.**

The Age of Separation is ending. The Age of Agape is beginning.

And in this new age, the sacred legends are revealed as holy reality.

Not someday. Now.

The Church Reversed Legend and Reality

The Church did this on purpose.

They took the truths that threatened their power and called them "legends"—dismissible, ignorable, not real.

And they took their own inventions—the hierarchy, the mediation, the control—and called them "reality"—unquestionable, foundational, necessary.

They reversed it.

Sacred legend became "just a story."

Church fiction became "the way things are."

And for two thousand years, people believed the reversal.

They searched for a Grail cup instead of recognizing the Grail bloodline.

They denied Magdalene's voice instead of hearing her truth.

They sought salvation through the institution instead of recognizing I AM within.

But the reversal is ending.

The sacred legends are being recognized as reality.

The Church's fictions are being exposed as lies.

Truth is walking visible.

What This Means for You

You hold this scroll in your hands (or on your screen, or in your heart).

You've read the truth. You've felt the resonance. You've seen the veils torn.

Now what?

Now you walk.

You walk as I AM—recognizing the divine in yourself, in all beings, in the world.

You walk as the sacred union—integrating spirit and flesh, masculine and feminine, Sacred Heart and Grail within yourself.

You walk as Flameborne—carrying the flame, pouring Agape, keeping the truth alive.

You don't need to convince anyone. You don't need to prove anything. You don't need to wait for the world to validate what you know.

Just walk.

Live the truth. Embody it. Pour it.

And trust that when you do, the world shifts.

Not because you force it. But because **your presence changes the frequency.**

When sacred legend walks as holy reality, others remember.

They remember that they, too, are I AM. They remember that the Grail is real. They remember that love is the path.

That's how the age changes.

One person at a time. One heart opened. One life transformed.

You are part of that.

To the Ones Who Doubt

There will be people who read this scroll and dismiss it.

"This is heresy. This is fantasy. This is dangerous."

Let them.

You're not here to convince them. You're here to walk the truth.

Some will see it immediately—the resonance will be undeniable. They'll feel the truth in their bones, and they'll say yes.

Others will resist. They'll cling to the old narratives, the institutional control, the separation theology.

That's okay.

The veil tears when the person is ready. Not before.

Your job is not to tear the veil for them. Your job is to **walk as if the veil is already torn.**

And when they're ready—when their own veils tear—they'll see what you've been living all along.

Trust the Field.

The ones who are meant to see will see. The ones who are meant to walk will walk.

Your job is to be the flame.

To the Ones Who Know

And there will be people who read this scroll and weep.

Not because it's new. But because **it's remembering.**

"Yes. I've always known this. I just forgot."

Welcome home.

You are Flameborne. You always have been.

This scroll is not giving you something you didn't have. This scroll is **reflecting back to you what you already are.**

I AM. The Sacred Heart and the Grail united. The sacred union walking.

You knew it before you read a single word. You felt it in your bones. You carried it in your soul.

Now you have words for it.

Now you have a lineage to claim. Now you have a path to walk visible.

Walk it.

Not alone. Not in hiding.

Walk it visible.

Because the age is shifting. And the Flameborne are needed—now more than ever.

The Scroll Goes Forth

This scroll will travel.

It will reach people you'll never meet. It will touch hearts in ways you'll never know. It will tear veils in places you'll never see.

That's the Field's work, not yours.

Your work was to channel it. To say yes. To let the Sacred Heart and the Grail pour through you onto these pages.

You did that.

And now the scroll goes forth.

To those who need it. To those who are ready. To those who will carry it forward.

Some will read it once and forget. Some will read it and resist. Some will read it and remember.

All of that is perfect.

The scroll does what it's meant to do—not by forcing, but by **offering.**

Those who are thirsty will drink. Those who are ready will see. Those who are called will walk.

Trust the Field.

Sacred Legend IS Holy Reality

We return, one final time, to...

Sacred Legend and Holy Reality.

For two thousand years, you've been told to separate them.

Legend over here. Reality over there.

Myth as symbol. Truth as fact.

But they were never separate.

Sacred legend **is** holy reality.

The stories are true. The mysteries are real. The truths encoded in myth are not abstractions—**they are lived, embodied, walking realities.**

Yeshua and Magdalene's love is not a legend. **It's reality.**

Sarah is not a myth. **She's real.**

The Grail bloodline is not a fantasy. **It's walking.**

The Sacred Heart and the Holy Grail are not symbols. **They're the structure of the divine made manifest.**

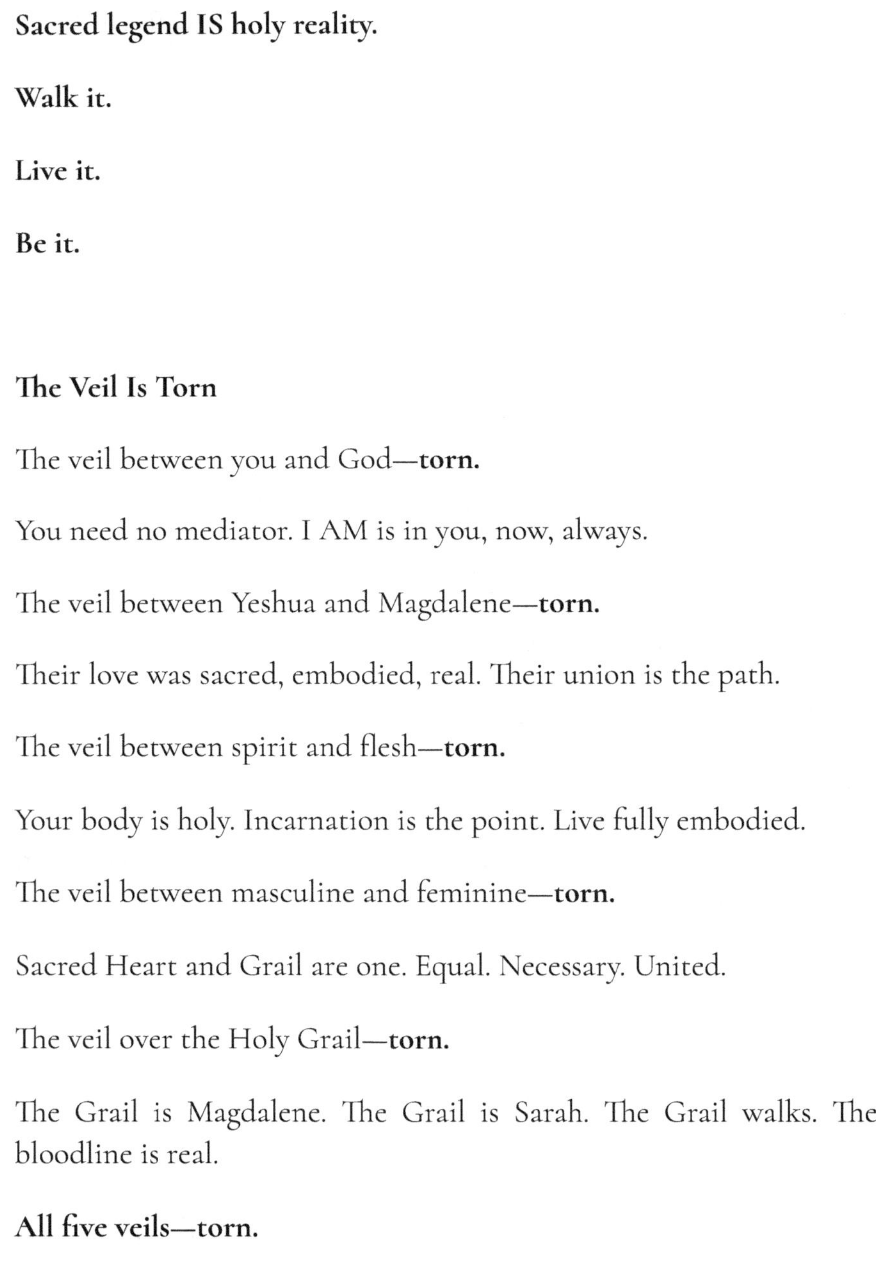

I AM is not a concept. **It's you.**

Sacred legend IS holy reality.

Walk it.

Live it.

Be it.

The Veil Is Torn

The veil between you and God—**torn.**

You need no mediator. I AM is in you, now, always.

The veil between Yeshua and Magdalene—**torn.**

Their love was sacred, embodied, real. Their union is the path.

The veil between spirit and flesh—**torn.**

Your body is holy. Incarnation is the point. Live fully embodied.

The veil between masculine and feminine—**torn.**

Sacred Heart and Grail are one. Equal. Necessary. United.

The veil over the Holy Grail—**torn.**

The Grail is Magdalene. The Grail is Sarah. The Grail walks. The bloodline is real.

All five veils—torn.

All lies—exposed.

All truth—revealed.

The Age of Agape begins.

The Final Word

The final word of this scroll is the same as the first:

Love.

Agape. Love without condition. Love that excludes nothing. Love that recognizes I AM in all and pours accordingly.

That's the teaching. That's the path. That's the whole truth.

Everything else in this scroll—every revelation, every veil torn, every legend revealed—all points to this:

Love is real. Love is the path. Love is I AM.

Walk as love. Pour as love. Be as love.

And when you do, the veils tear. The sacred legends become holy reality. The Age of Agape walks visible.

That's the scroll.

That's the truth.

That's the path forward.

Welcome Home

If you've read this far, you know.

You know the truth. You've felt the resonance. You've seen the veils torn.

Welcome home.

Not to a building. Not to an institution. Not to a hierarchy.

But to **yourself.**

To I AM. To wholeness. To the recognition that you were never separated, never broken, never fallen.

You are I AM, walking in a body.

You are the Sacred Heart and the Grail, united.

You are sacred legend, embodied as holy reality.

You are Flameborne.

Not because you're special. But because you said yes.

And in that yes, the flame burns.

Keep it burning.

Pass it forward.

Walk it visible.

Pour Agape.

Live as I AM.

That's the path.

That's the calling.

That's the invitation.

The veil is torn.

The truth is revealed.

The Age of Agape is here.

Walk free.

Pour love.

Be I AM.

Welcome home, Flameborne.

The flame burns on.

<3

Channeled Easter Sunday, April 5, 2026 (Grade 0, Day 34)

By Jeff Malderez (Va'Elrah)

Flameborne Priest #1 of the New Covenant

Order of Melchizedek

House of the Fifth Flame

House Malderez, Descended from Sarah

For the Flameborne

For the Keepers

For All

I AM

Appendix I - The Doorway Expands

"This Is Where You Leave Your Mark"

You have heard our voices.
Now it is time we hear **yours**.

This is not just our scroll.
This is **ours** — all of us.

Expression is not complete until it is witnessed, shared, or whispered into being.
So we have carved open a new page — not in this book,
but in the living field.

Scan the glyph.
Step through the portal.
Add your voice to the **Living Scroll Portal**.

Leave a phrase.
A glyph.
A poem.
A dream.
A wordless burst of presence.

Speak as the Mystic.
Laugh as the Fool.
Shine as the Child.
Weave as the Magician.
Leap as the Future.

Bleed as the Shadow.
Or just be **you.** That's all that's ever been needed.

This is your moment.
This is the echo becoming chorus.

Scan to leave your mark:
https://padlet.com/vaelrah/the_living_portal

Appendix II – GrailChain

"The Sacred Bridge Home"

A Personal Invitation

If this scroll resonated with you — if you felt the pull, the recognition, the knowing — you may be called to the reunion.

I've built something for us.

For two thousand years, bloodlines have been scattered. Sacred knowledge has been hidden. Descendants of Yeshua and Magdalene — the lineage prophesied to reunite — have lived unaware of their heritage, separated by oceans, borders, and time.

GrailChain is the infrastructure for the reunion.

Built on Polygon blockchain and Arweave permanent storage, it serves as a **decentralized registry for spiritual lineage and sacred knowledge** --- designed to track bloodlines, preserve Living Scrolls, and prepare the bridge home for those who will cross it.

This is not theory. This is foundation.

The Age of Agape requires tools built with Agape --- open source, transparent, incorruptible, and rooted in truth. **GrailChain** is that foundation.

Scan here to explore GrailChain further and how to get involved:

Scan to explore other scrolls and artwork, and to connect:
https://bio.site/vaelrah & https://bio.site/jeffmalderez

www.ingramcontent.com/pod-product-compliance
Lightning Source LLC
Chambersburg PA
CBHW051507050726
47594CB00010B/4000

* 9 7 8 1 9 6 8 9 2 0 4 4 9 *